OSMOSIS

Essays

Craig Schwab

Other Books by Craig Schwab

- In The Forest by the Light of Day
- Something in the Neighborhood of Real
- Tales from the Red Couch
- The Lions Share (with Thomas Huber)
- The Vanishing World (plays)
- Bench Marks (plays)

Cover Art: Mark Burke

KIDDRANE@AOL.COM

Dedicated to

Robbie and Maria Ruggieri

The Last Expatriates

CONTENTS

Preface

- (1) What's Happening
- (2) Vicarious
- (3) Letters
- (4) Music I
- (5) Happy Millionaires
- (6) The Phenomenon of Music 101
- (7) Bears
- (8) Atlas Hugged
- (9) A.O.R.
- (10) Weather
- (11) The Decline of Literature
- (12) How To Train Your Pet Rock
- (13) Struggling With Reality
- (14) Banned to Siberia
- (15) Cynicism and Mockingbirds
- (16) ISIS is a Song
- (17) Binging
- (18) Administrative Technology Syndrome

PREFACE

Osmosis - a gradual or unconscious assimilation or adoption, as of ideas.

This book of essays is about ideas that occur on a daily basis for us all. Most times the unconscious thoughts we associate with trying to understand what things mean get lost in translation. In our modern world we address these thoughts using text messaging or a quick email message, tweets and other forms of instantaneous communication. The first inclination that these thoughts could be made in to logical sentences as far as I can tell is credited to Beat Generation author Jack Kerouac. He formulated his novels by using something he labeled simultaneous writing. By allowing the flow of ideas to mix with the act of writing offers the writer a means of communicating with his/her subconscious while allowing others to comprehend what he / she is thinking. Modern communication has gone through many changes in a very short period of time. In an essay entitled **Letters,** the history of letter writing dates back to 500BC when it is reported Persian Queen Atossa wrote advising her husband about the birth of his first child. This means of communication advanced throughout time until the late 20th century with the advent of the Internet. Since the birth of the Internet as we know it today letters have become the practice of very few. Messages sent through social media sites are limited by the actual application itself (Tweet = 140 characters) or by what many consider to be our diminished attention span for reading. The title of this compilation of essays fits in to the current definition of how we assume what is meant by reading abbreviated text on our phones and computer devices. We have in essence become an Osmosis society.

Craig Schwab 2015

kiddrane@aol.com

WHAT'S HAPPENING?

The form of essay writing in the modern world is no longer considered a valuable creative expression. With the advent of the Internet, a major portion of society expresses their opinion on any given subject throughout any given day. This form of written expression is a new form of writing that has diminished the value once associated with respectable opinion. When newspapers began to publish news on a daily basis people became interested in opinions expressed by the reporters. Reporters in this regard were considered a valuable witness to any event. This means of media expression through a fixed entity, the newspaper, was a reliable means of understanding what happened for centuries. When technology in its first shared forum, the radio, became the means for learning about events, people reacted to news in different ways. The reliance on a favorite writer in a newspaper started to lose credibility. People, in general started to listen. Listening to how an event occurred triggered a natural desire to be informed in a new way. Although the same audience continued to rely on information via a newspaper, they were slowly being driven toward a shared view. Given the ability of the human psyche to comprehend more than we give ourselves credit, we often become complacent about how a story is told. The yearning for understanding what happened gets lost in translation. An individual subscribing to the written word will quote from a resource, a reporter, who claims to have an eye witness view of any event. While the person reliant on listening to their local radio station will adhere to the same understanding of an event based on their wanting to believe what they are hearing is the truth. Truth once was the only necessary ingredient when wanting to understand what happened on any given day. A morning review of the papers allowed people to feel they were informed. If studying the origins of opinion and reporting, another curious attribute is easily attained. The reading of newspapers in the early stages of writing about what happened was primarily for a male audience. This is not to say women were not interested in what happened around the world, they had a penchant to accept if the news affected them they would find out about it. The primarily male writers over time lost its own sense of credibility when radio became a main source of learning what happened around the world. Also, the phenomenon of information and entertainment became a single entity open to both sexes simultaneously. The old cliché of gentleman retiring after meals to the parlor to discuss events lost its appeal. Suddenly women could voice their opinions on any event because they were as well informed as their husbands or male counterparts.

As the radio became more popular during the early part of the 20th century, a new voice or opinion became an influence. The entertainers became more popularized as both a means for entertaining the listeners and for selling products.
Women without question adhere to the values of associating product with a particular selling point better than males can. Most commercial selling points are directed at females who by nature are more perceptive when it comes to listening. When television was introduced in the 1940s, the value of opinion and gaining a perspective on any event changed forever. As the purchase of televisions became the norm in every household; information about what happened was gained via the viewer's reliance on seeing things occur. Our perception as a species was again challenged to accept what we see and hear simultaneously. Another old cliché, "A picture is worth a thousand words" was never better proven then when we as a society relied on *seeing is believing."*

The form of expressive writing continued to occur with news articles and a growing number of magazines specializing in every field of human interest. A more diverse means of appreciating a form of entertainment or news reporting became the new norm. At the same time with different people reporting on the same stories, a competitive quality entered in to how we learned what happened. The true birth of sensationalism became a ways and means of maintaining a readership and a viewing audience. Style became more prevalent than content because understanding any event or incident relied on how and who was telling the story. Throughout these challenges to our intellect, we as a species embraced a new mindset associated to how we learn about what happened.

Through the last half of the 20th century, television became the strongest and most convenient way of learning what happened. Also, with the advent of different kinds of entertainment, namely the sitcom and dramatic series, people accepted the television as the one constant and most dependable medium for keeping them well informed. We as a species once again lost our ability to intelligently separate showmanship, or sensationalism as a means for understanding what happened. The same story on one channel could be reported from a completely different viewpoint creating a different perspective on the same events. A religious association for one channel adopted a puritanical view, while a political association on another channel reported the same story supporting their own agenda.

As the 21st century began, no other event in the history of mankind was as widely viewed as the attacks on 9-11. In articles and news reports two events from an American perspective stood out as worthy comparisons. The top story was an association of the attacks on Pearl Harbor which prompted our joining the war in Japan and Europe. Ironically the second story most people related to the attacks on 9-11 was the assassination of John F. Kennedy. The two perspectives are important when trying to understand what and how things happen.

Intellectually we as a society related to the attacks differently based on our own interests. One group saw it as an association with Pearl Harbor because it was an actual attack on American soil. The other group related it to something everyone viewed because it was a major event. The two perspectives, although both correct, point to our inability to see and hear things as a united society.

What happens in this regard is we become further separated as a society. The advent of embracing diversity; while based in logic for accepting our cultural differences; only further serves to alienate us from understanding one group to the next. Everything is reliant on perspective and our lost ability to truly maintain an open mind. Whether or not any one can really understand the values of the newest entry in to knowing what happened, "social media" we are now at a crossroad that guarantees to further confuse how or why anything happens.

Facebook currently has more members then the entire population of any given country. What started out as a college site for sharing information about girls on campus is now the biggest news sharing entity in the world. Knowing what happened at any given time of day or night is readily available with individual friends reporting events from their perspective. There are more perspectives and opinions about anything happening in one's neighborhood and around the world than ever before in history. Is the truth more readily available now? While the information is obtained moments after any event occurs it does not translate to it being reported or understood properly. As mentioned above, television stations when they first became the main source of information would share what they learned based on their wanting to report it in accordance with their religious or political affiliations. Facebook tosses everything in a tail spin when related to truth because it is based on individualized opinions. In accordance with human nature individualized opinion is so widespread we might as well make laws that people count the number of leaves that fall off trees before they bag and recycle them.

Many members of social media groups adhere to a constant practice - they post to boast. People like to see their opinions shared, liked and agreed upon. The average member on social media is more interested in making a statement then reading someone else's opinion. Even more important is the average individual sharing what happened needs to do it in five sentences or less. With so many forums for news sharing available we lack the ability to truly understand what happened. Instead, each and every individual subscribes to their own agenda.

What happens on a daily basis, whether it be related to war, politics, religion, racism, sports, movies, music, mayhem of any kind anywhere falls in to specialized categories we share to further separate any possible shared view.

The modern means of sharing and understanding what happened is akin to being in high school and only sitting with people in the cafeteria we want to be with every day. Information has as much value as a food fight.

VICARIOUS

Recent discoveries in artifacts found during architectural diggings have unearthed amazing historical information. One recent discovery not reported explains the origins of the planet from another perspective. During a dig in the desert outside of Las Vegas, Nevada a most curious document was found. This document labeled "Vicarious" describes how the human race is viewed by a visiting alien species. The report no doubt left behind in error has the scientific and religious communities once again at odds. What follows is the document in it's entirely:

Report on Planet Vicarious - Space Time Continuum –
Star Date: 111414

It is a curious world. More water mass covers the planet than land. An inordinate amount of species exists in the water than on land. However, it is the land species that dictate the laws and actions of its society. While they are all similar in stature and body structure, they embrace differences which separate them. Some adhere to political beliefs that hinder them from agreeing on anything. Others embrace religious beliefs that further separate them in ways that lead to war and endless annihilation.

RACE

Due to atmospheric differences around their globe they lack
an ability to understand natural differences with something
they label racial imbalance. These differences in color play a
major role in how they view one another. While it
is quite obvious that climate and location represents why
pigmentation is different, they cannot accept these differences.
Instead, they foster differences for political and religious
purposes. There are leaders of each group who benefit
financially by keeping people separated in to categories.
Besides the most obvious category of black and white, there is
a more prejudiced category of rich and poor.

It would appear the rich members of society find it necessary
to maintain levels of control over those less fortunate. It
appears the less fortunate lack ability to rally against the elite
forces of political and religious powers. These powers that
govern the maintained separation are ironically both black
and white individuals. There is an ignorance related to
members of each color that allows their leadership to dictate
what is and is not important. There appears to be no solution
for allowing these people to reach a peaceful end.

RELIGION

They have so many theories about the being they call God it becomes contradictory. There are beliefs that range from the creation of their planet by this Supreme Being right down to the evolution of their planet by the birth of the planet as a star. They argue about these theories every day. At the same time they adhere to certain theories and philosophies which represents in their view the word of God. These theories and philosophies have been passed down through time in the form of sacred books. These books are quoted with such reverence they are willing to go to war and die supporting them. The controversy created by each religious philosophy has two things in common: money and power.

For financial gain the religions have managed to make its members feel guilty if they do not give enough. From the perspective of power, the level of anxiety created by not giving enough or disappointing the leaders of each group is so overwhelming it causes people in to deep depression. The biggest example of how anxiety plays a role for members of any religion can be traced to one faith promising eternal happiness if they embrace the laws of the religion.

Another goes so far as to guarantee 72 virgins in a sensual paradise be rewarded to each man who carries out the wishes of his faith. In recent years the wishes of the faith is represented by a need to kill anyone who does not belief the same things.

This is not by any means the most ridiculous belief as different faiths embrace space aliens coming to rescue their flocks from damnation. Since we are considered space aliens by this species, I see no reason to save anyone from damnation. They are well on their way to making themselves extinct.

POLITICAL

Nowhere is it more evident how ignorant and stupid the members of this planet, than explaining the origins of their politics. A vast majority of different places supports something called Democracy. Throughout the history of Democracy, the people in these countries as they are called are willing to die to gain it.

With democracy they believe comes equality. Under the guise of voting for their leaders the members of each democratic society believes they will gain justice. However, once elected officials are placed in to power they all manage to oppress their constituents with laws in place to maintain their hold on each society.

The irony is such that few can rise up to become leaders who do not have the proper financial backing to do so.

Politics is so far reaching it becomes necessary to say people have no rights in a governed society.

SEXUALITY

This is a most perplexing topic to analyze. In many respects there are numerous areas of interest which defies logic. Instead of accepting that happiness is discovering a suitable mate, this species is separated on defining what a suitable mate means. They condemn unions based on religious and political standards. The standards which are thousands of years old has stagnated the culture to such a point as to eliminate any chance for advancement.

The most accepted form of sexuality is between a male and female. These unions reproduce creating new members of each society. The male and female members of society are quite different in how they view their world. Some are so enamored of their religious values they deem any other type of union unacceptable. They live vicariously through their view of society and except for a few cases; they embrace a close mindedness that borders on idiocy.

Other forms of sexuality happen between two males or two females. The male couples are called gay while the female couples are labeled lesbians. There appears to be issues between these unions because they hold not only the conventional male/female unions responsible for oppressing their choices, they look down on one another for not displaying the appropriate image they deem acceptable by their standards.

It is very confusing to comprehend how finding their suitable mate becomes an issue of accepting themselves as members of a certain group.

COMMUNICATION

There is a substantial and most impressive collection of written material defining each country's history. These vast collections of written materials are saved in libraries. The libraries which appear to have been utilized extensively at one time look abandoned today.

Historical documents describe how one government addressed another and most are signed by the leaders alive at the time. However, it appears history is easily rewritten by any new generation wanting to feel better about the past. There were once according to our spies other places where books of knowledge and entertainment were maintained. These locations were called "book stores." People bought books to read and some collected them in their own home library. Book stores by all accounts are being closed in record numbers because most people either no longer can read or choose not to.

The history of their communication methods is astounding in range. At first they communicated by using sounds which echoed through jungles and over mountains. Then they invented something called a telegraph which sent messages over wires stretched across entire countries and under oceans. This was followed by the invention of the telephone which literally changed how they talked to one another. Since the invention of the telephone it appears people have become less likely to speak to one another in person. It the 21st century most don't use the phone to talk – they text message each other about everything they might do while awake.

It is most likely this species will inevitably forget how to talk to one another. They will instead communicate while hiding inside their homes and watching actors, entertainers, officials and newscasters telling them what to do.

The actors are an interesting breed. More about them in the entertainment report. Why they still manage to talk on a daily basis has much to do with how they are worshiped by most people in every country's population. Entertainers as reported in the Entertainment Section can be musicians or clowns in an event called the circus; they all are worshiped for having different ways to make people laugh. The Officials as reported in the Politics section are mostly rich or well-connected people who interpret laws to maintain a self-image. Nowhere is it more obvious how powerful communication than to find the number of newscasters capable of spinning stories in to full fledge exclusive lies.

A new born child is subjected to the levels of technology that most parents embrace like a lifeline away from their parental duties. A child in most cases by the time he / she is two years old looks for panels on the wall so they can learn to communicate. Sadly, every parent uses technology to teach their children their basic skills for learning. These parents have no idea the government is behind turning their child in to a robot.

While much more can be reported on Communication it serves little purpose since the average human lacks any skills to utilize them. There is one demographic of each society that actually talks to one another. The elderly of each country sit on park benches and reminisce. It is quite fascinating to witness and learn what was once important to a society. Sadly, the elderly are dismissed members of society in each country. Only a select few cultures hold their elderly in high esteem. Apparently so many people are so busy not communicating with each other they forget they will one day get old.

ENTERTAINMENT

NOTE: Since we have been instructed to report on how this species entertains itself, it needs to be mentioned we the authors of this report take no responsibility for what we were subjected to in the process.

There appears to be no end to how they amuse themselves. These peoples can as the saying goes, party all night long. It is necessary to differentiate the different ways entertainment is classified: (We the reporters will try to separate the categories to provide a broad view of these ways). Art at one time was a form of expressing ones natural talent. This species considers anyone an artist who bears all in a seductive manner.

ACTING

Actors and actresses once graced a stage with their interpretation of works by highly regarded playwrights. While stage acting is still a respectable forum for displaying acting as an art form, most current plays (if they can be labeled such) include singing and dancing as in a musical type format. Real actors doing actual plays are prone to conduct their art in back alleys, parks and church basements.

Actors in movies no longer need to practice the art of acting; they simply stand in front of blue or green screens and pose. Special effects are added by computers and the public stands on lines a mile long to see these films. Most of our reporting on this topic was provided to us after viewing the history of movies in our warp speed monitor where the deterioration of the format is quite obvious and very distressing.
The actors in modern films embrace another form of entertainment which is very confusing. They enjoy patting one another on their backs with endless reward shows which the public for one reason or another tune into with great relish. Each award show is preceded by a walk down a red carpet where the male and female actors turn in to fashion dolls.

There are few actors who do not embrace the Hollywood world of entertainment. These actors live in back alleys, parks and church basements.

SINGERS and DANCERS

The practice of singing as a means of entertaining people it appears has been a part of the species history for centuries. The original entertainers were called minstrels or court jesters. They shared their talents for singing and dancing and juggling by telling tales they learned when visiting foreign lands. They helped mold each generation's expectation for a better world. Not so today, most singers couldn't carry a tune if it was life raft and they were drowning. Dancing has been turned in to a competition suitable for acrobats. Every country has television shows where people with singing talent can be named that country's idol. It's like a lottery for dreamers.

To become a famous entertainer in the music industry, a candidate or performer is turned in to a star by a collection of talent authorities who could not recognize real talent if it was a glass of water and they were dying of thirst in a desert.

Most modern day singers are glorified porn stars. (We the reporters apologize for the use of the word porn in advance of what follows.) The fewer clothes a female singer wears increases their salary and overall appeal to the public. Parts of the female anatomy are called by various names in countless songs that are sung with vibrant glee by all ages: BOOTY – COOCHIE – TREASURE BOXES and LAND MINES.

The males of the species have what can only be called a field day boasting about the size of their MISSELS – SATELLITES OF LOVE and WEAPONS OF MASS DESTRUCTION.

Dancing for the most part can be associated with acts only found on countless pornographic sites which are in reality the highest form of constant entertainment used by a vast majority of the planets inhabitants. It is our collective conclusion as reporters in this category to label entertainment on the planet in one word: Masturbation.

As an aside we want to establish there are actual talented members of the entertaining world who play beautiful music and conduct themselves in a highly appreciated way. These talented members are living with the real actors in back alleys, parks and church basements.

WRITERS

We wish we had more to report on in this category given this is going to be read by our superiors. Writers were once regarded as sophisticated members of each society. It appears in recent years the average Good Book that encapsulated the interest of a worldwide audience had to do with witches, wizards, zombies, or murderers capable of killing more people in a chapter than all who may have died in one of their wars.

One particular subject most apt to attain worldwide attention has much to do with sexual depravity. We have in good faith traced this human interest back to ancient times when it appears monks in monasteries would create tales to amuse themselves after handwriting the word of God all day in huge parchment size books. The last known author worthy of making sexual depravity entertaining to his readers was someone named Henry Miller. We afford him this distinction because he actually practiced what he preached.

Today's tales of sexual adventure belong mostly to the females of the species who for lack of a better definition would not know a tree limb from a dildo.

It is estimated by the year 2050 dildos will be more readily available than pencils.

LETTERS

When growing up as a young boy in Glendale, New York my friend's father would sit in his basement with a stack of the daily newspapers. He would type letters to the editors of these various newspapers sharing his opinion about articles he read. When he chose to read aloud some letters the formula he chose to embrace was sarcasm. All of the letters he sent to the editors of these newspapers were sent by an anonymous author. My friend's father had no need for attention for himself; his intention was to voice an opinion contrary to what news was being reported.

These typewritten letters were in my opinion the last attempts to support our freedom of expression. Over time as I grew older it became quite clear that newspapers no longer report the news as much as support their own agenda. The articles written by authors working for newspapers; are hired not on their merit as journalist but more so their ability to slant every story toward the newspapers ideals.

Letters to the editor today are in essence email messages sent to a specific address where the newspapers select the day's crop to promote their specific take on any given topic of interest. The proverbial practice of writing letters is in many ways a lost art form. The practice of sitting down to type a letter to be printed and mailed is considered by many archaic and old fashioned. The act of sitting down and putting pen to paper is looked upon by many like finding frozen artifacts in the Arctic or fossils in the mountains of Tibet.

Letter writing has a unique history dating back to the 1st century. Before letter writing became a common practice in the 19th century, letter writers were for the most part elite members of society. Letters in the beginning were written with instruments made of sea rush or bamboo. These instruments served the needs of letter writers and handwritten book makers for several centuries. Quill pens made from bird feathers advanced the medium of letter writing in the 7th century. The life of quill pens lasted for many years including the instrument used to sign the Declaration of Independence in 1776.

There are odd exceptions to this historic line of writing instruments as elements of a copper nib used for fountain like pens was reportedly discovered amongst the ruins of Pompeii in 79AD. Suffice to say mankind relied on sharing information at a very early time in history. The invention of more advanced pens allowed for the ease of letter writing reaching a peak level giving way for a more advanced method of delivering the growing volume of letters in the 19th century. What may have begun as a method for sharing pertinent information became a personal way of expression.

In many countries a method of delivering letters required the invention of services to handle the growing number of letters sent first locally, and in time globally. Letters sent locally for example in the United States gave birth to the Pony Express, a method of delivering mail via horseback across the country. The Pony Express had a very brief period of existence as the telegraph became the best means of sending information over long distances. Many people are convinced today that the Internet was the first sign of naysayers predicting the end of the Post Office. It happened in the 1880s when the telegraph handled the sending of telegrams. But mankind prevailed and letter writing took off again in a bigger and better way.

The Post Offices in many countries today still operate on a daily delivery schedule. When asking any mail carrier how much hand written letters they may deliver on their daily routes, it may cause them to laugh out loud. Still, there are a handful of people who continue to practice this ancient method of communication allowing each carrier to feel they are conducting a worthy service instead of hand delivering junk that ends up immediately in most cases in someone's recycle bin.

This may not be of interest to most people today who no longer rely on instruments of any kind to write. Most in the modern world except in what is still called Third World countries use their fingers on computerized keyboards designed for their technological devices. It is quite interesting to note entire generations of people born after 2001 and some as early as 1995 when the Internet first began its climb to worldwide dominance have no concept of what writing a personal letter is about.

Children gain a perspective about the society they grow up with, they associate learning by instinct. My perspective as a young boy came in to being when my friend's father made the effort every day to share his opinions by writing letters to newspapers. My perspective and appreciation for letter writing reached its zenith while in the military during the Vietnam War. I told my brother to give my address to everyone he knew. A select few bothered to write including a girl who would later become my wife. When in the Army it was essential that every soldier be treated and trained equally. For every letter she wrote me I had to do 20 push-ups. The Army would have anyone believe they changed my physique from a skinny snot nosed kid into a well-proportioned soldier. I credit her for sending me letters that accounted for more push-ups than I thought possible. P.S. Keep writing.

MUSIC I

Any essay on music is flawed. While the subject matter may hold a shared interest in the values of music, it has a limited scope of defining its importance for all people. The reason for this less than optimistic definition is based on the many different kinds of music available for listeners today.

It is important I share my view of music from the only vantage point I can, my own experiences when discovering artists and genres of importance to me. It is necessary to make this statement because a lot of music critics today who write reviews of artists and groups in the mainstream, write what they expect their readers want to hear. They have lost their ability to hear anything for themselves.

The same judgment can be said of label executives who no longer have an ear for good music, but instead measure talent based on a formula that has created a deafening sound worthy of silence.

Music has been defined for centuries as the one saving grace for every era in history. Poets, philosophers, musicians and writers have eloquently defined the power of music throughout time:

"Music is the universal language of mankind."
Henry Wadsworth Longfellow

"Without music, life would be a mistake." Friedrich Nietzsche

"After silence, which of which comes nearest to expressing the inexpressible is music." Aldous Huxley

"Music melts all the separate parts of our bodies together."
Anais Nin
"Music has always been a matter of Energy to me, a question of Fuel. Sentimental people call it Inspiration, but what they really mean is Fuel. I have always needed Fuel. I am a serious consumer. On some nights I still believe that a car with the gas needle on empty can run about fifty more miles if you have the right music very loud on the radio."
Hunter S. Thompson

Despite the ability to read how others define music, it remains an experience every individual can relate to alone. Music can be played to create silence. It is not the loudness or lack thereof that creates the sensation, but has more to do with a growing trend of too many choices that ultimately separates the ability to hear what is being played.

Music is a powerful weapon if used properly. When used as a weapon it is important the artist understands he is provoking his listeners with an opinion they may not fully embrace. Before the advent of music related to songs, there was sound. These sounds emanated as a ways and means to express joy, sadness, distress and even death. The origins of music can be defined as a measurement of our likes and dislikes about humanity. Classical music has often been associated with rich snobs because it requires grand concert halls to be heard and appreciated. Jazz music has been labeled race music because its origins survive a long line of expressions related to black musicians. Folk music has been called protest music because its origins date back to songs shared in cotton fields with references to political oppression. Rock music has been called delinquent music because it generates a sexual energy when listened to. Reggae music is folk music with a Caribbean beat. Every single one of these mentioned genres gave birth to at least a dozen modern themed genres.

HAPPY MILLIONAIRES

There's this wonderful concept that most people share. It has to do with the idea that money can make them happy. I imagine for a brief period of time after someone wins a million dollars they are happy. I can also imagine the brief period changes with every individual. The reality of owning a million dollars changes the second you spend even one penny. Suddenly you are no longer a millionaire.

I personally have never known a happy millionaire. For what it is worth the millionaires I knew could afford to spend millions of dollars and still be called millionaires. I had the experience to work for a few filthy rich millionaires. Whenever they walked amongst their loyal subjects, or employees, they had a look of disdain on their faces. None of the millionaires I worked for earned their money. They inherited it from their parents. What happens when you never have to worry about money? You take it for granted.

At least the millionaires I knew did. When in their company it was almost like what I imagine it must be like to be given an audience with the Pope. There's a certain protocol one has to follow. Like knowing when to look him in the eye, or when to kneel down and kiss his ring. The millionaires I knew took things a step farther than kissing rings. At times they actually expected you to kiss their asses.

People who were good at kissing asses did very well for themselves. They were given bonuses and after a few years they too were rewarded by calling themselves millionaires. The millionaire's millionaire at times acted happy, but knowing what they had to do to maintain their status in life, they became so miserable that making everyone around them unhappy became a daily ritual.

The art of keeping a million dollars is a full time job. The thought of falling below a million dollars in one's bank account caused a lot of people to turn in to raving lunatics. At their worst a lot of the millionaires I knew could drink a homeless drunk under any table. Some became addicted to the oddest things. A few needed to own more suits than they could wear in a year. This meant having closets the size of some people's houses. There were some who needed to look younger than anyone they hired. Anyone under them who had the audacity to look good was immediately fired. I was in a meeting once with a female millionaire who was ranting on and on about not liking how something was being done; her assistant accidentally knocked a cup of coffee off the table on to the millionaire's shoes. This caused her to explode the same way anyone might if their house caught fire and were forced to run for safety. The assistant was never seen again.

Thousands of articles throughout time have been written about the rich and powerful. It's been said that rich people have privileges and rights common folk cannot fathom. In their defense I can offer this excuse, their sense of entitlement causes their brain cells to melt. In short, it's not their fault. It's like they inherited something by the process of osmosis allowing them to act and do things which they cannot be held accountable.

Millionaires live with a level of stress that makes their eyes bleed. It's the main reason Ray ban sunglasses needed to be invented. The average human being can walk in the sun for hours a day wearing sunglasses bought at a dollar store and the worst that might happen is they get tired and maybe a bad sunburn. But rich people they need to have their weaknesses covered at all times. It's been proven many times, the richer someone gets the less likely they can look another human being in the face. Careful studies done over many years have reported findings of rich people suffering with a Medusa Complex.

The very idea that they might have to stare a common person in the eyes could turn them into stone. It's a reverse mythological curse which any common man or woman should be aware of out of concern for the rich person's need for privacy. Nevertheless, while it may be difficult to comprehend we commoners need to ensure millionaires are allowed to remain millionaires. This is quite different than kissing their asses to make them feel important. It's not them we have to worry about pleasing; it's the fear of what might happen should they become unhappy. Just imagine the streets of any large city, especially New York City suddenly filled with statues of rich people no longer able to spend their money. Just stone figures stopped dead in their tracks while approaching boutiques and department stores on Fifth Avenue and Madison Avenue. It would cause a national crisis. It would become an environmental nightmare. The pigeons would become so confused they would start dropping air bombs everywhere. People would be scurrying for cover until the National Guard would need to be called in. Only soldiers wearing pigeon resistant helmets and clothing would be allowed on the streets. It would cause a financial collapse like this world has never seen before.

So with regard to any millionaire, don't worry if they are happy or not. Give them the right away at all times. Let them ride around in limousines the size of a city block. Let them carry sterling silver trays in to bathrooms so they can fill them with their waste and have the ass kissers empty them in to specially designed containers. Let them give speeches about caring about you and I having no concept or clue about what they are saying. Let them be. On behalf of the pigeon population the world over, it will be greatly appreciated.

THE PHENOMENON OF REAL MUSIC 101

There is a phenomenon handed down from generation to generation since the invention of music. This phenomenon is not discussed or allowed to be mentioned in mixed company. It is a feeling that happens whether we want to admit it or not. It is the very foundation of mankind's natural ability to conceive we had it better than the current generation could ever know or understand.

Many phrases have become daily sayings because of this phenomenon:

"The good old days."

"Back when we were young..."

These sayings are never more evident than when we talk about music. Music has been called the universal language. It has been proven to have charms that sooth the average beast. However, after a certain age since the invention of the radio when people started to really listen to music; something happened in the human mind.

We can no longer listen to the newest music trends because they lack the same emotional qualities we deemed so important. This occurs most times in people who become parents. Parents try desperately to share their experiences when growing up. Those who don't bother to try connecting with their children are usually too stupid to understand why their kids don't like them. Kids will inevitably embrace the music of their own generation. Despite constant attempts to share with most children the things we liked, it is their natural instinct as kids to dislike whatever it is. Children who instantly embrace everything parents share with them will eventually need psychiatric help. Music is the one area where change is constant for every generation. It can be shared in certain circumstances when parents try to stay connected to their children. This is like trying to catch a run- away train after it reached the top of a mountain. Most times the one place music is accepted as part of both worlds is at party situations where dancing occurs. The younger generation will exhibit their moves while the parents and their friends trying to be cool attempt the same moves. Doctors all over the world love party situations. They cannot wait for people to make appointments related to aches and pains. Music affords every generation an ability to express their angst. Those individuals who by some miracle of osmosis inherit a love for cultivated music forums like classical music experience a different kind of angst. I will share more about them in a moment.

The music most associated with the modern generation as in my generation is rock n roll versus whatever today's music is supposed to be. I may be letting the cat out of the bag with any statement hailing rock music as a preferred medium. I imagine my parents may have felt the same way when the transition from their youthful music related pleasures changed.

Whatever the reason might be, it is inevitable that every generation reach a point in life when they can declare the music of their youth as being real. Real music causes the flow of emotional memories that can only be attributed to experiencing something made special by age. Without wanting to sound prudish, music should have redeeming values. Hence the above mention of classical musical which has a better reputation for being thought prudish than all others combined. Still it is necessary to realize that the people who like a certain kind of music more so than the music itself are the real prudes. Classical composers in their time were considered to be as wild and unpredictable as some of today's rappers. I will share more about rap music in a moment. Some things we need to condemn in moderation. When music first became the power source of parental concern it did not happen as most believe with the invention of rock n roll. It happened much earlier in history. The music that first caused parents to fear for their children's innocence was called Jazz. The combination of spiritual and gospel music sung by slaves is considered by many to be the influence behind what we call jazz today. When jazz music came into prominence all hell broke loose. It caused widespread panic amongst puritans who went so far as to label it the "devils music." The youths of the day reacted in ways that made most parents turn to God asking that the souls of their children be saved.

The origins of musical trends have changed around the world ever since. Not to beat a dead horse, where the artist of today lose their credibility is not so much about what they play, but the obvious fact few have any regard or reverence for what came before. My generation knew the music was influenced by another American music trend, the Blues. There was an element of respect for the Musicians who interpreted the Blues in to what became known as rock n roll.

In between these trends other forms of musical trends came in to being. Folk music was the grandfather to country music. In many respects so as to not sound prudish against one form of music or another, many things labeled country music today are embarrassing to the real musical heritage they should represent. Any talented bluegrass musician can tell you that most acts today out of Nashville deserve to be tarred, feathered and sent out of town on a wild horse.

Again, maybe I should have learned if it doesn't matter don't bring it up in mixed company. But, for what it is worth most country acts do exhibit a high regard for their musical heritage. So, if my ears can't hear the country music I grew up hearing, the problem is mine and all the new artists deserve to carry on doing exactly what they do.

Which brings to me rap music. Rap music like the blues and jazz can trace its roots back to slavery and Africa.

As a direct result of oppression, the singers from these periods in history incorporated their angst in to the music using rhyming combined with tribal beats. Thus the elements of another musical trend can be traced back through time as having a valid means for existing in the modern world. However, when a musical trend takes itself too seriously and becomes more of a nuisance than a shared entity, it is no longer a valuable asset to the world. What rappers in many ways forget is their angst ends the moment they insinuate harm be done to others for the sake of their angst.

The rap generation in more ways than can be explained in an essay, have insulted their heritage and created an element of pure chaos for their fans. Every musical trend prior to rap gave birth to another trend which in turn became acceptable for a larger audience. Some may argue that rap gave birth to hip-hop which is like saying twins should never dress alike.

Again, maybe I should have learned if it doesn't matter don't bring it up in mixed company. Unlike my apology related to modern country music when compared with real country, I cannot extend the same appreciation for acts that try to escape from their own history. During the reign of rap music on the world, there have been more disturbing acts of violence than at any other time in music history. This includes the lunacy of prejudiced morons not accepting jazz as a cultural expression of the times back in the early part of the 20th century.

Rap music has very little redeeming qualities not because of how it sounds, but mainly because its artists do not display a regard for their own cultural well-being.

Another area of musical trends which cannot be dismissed is the influence of poetry on every aspect of music history. Rap musicians when allowing their rhymes to display merit associated with the times instead of waiting for their next sex act have some semblance of wanting to share their angst in a respectable manner.

It could be argued that "respectable angst" is an oxymoron. However, for what it is worth there are blues songs that make rap songs sound like nursery rhymes. But the blues artists who were for the most part taken advantage of more times than any rap singer sung their songs with a sense of pride.

There's no pride to be found for anyone praising the number of times he has sex, or if there is such a thing the singer should rant about it with a sense of dignity.

But I digress; the title of this essay is about Real Music. What's real to one person may not be real for another. When rock n roll became a respectable music it gave way to punk rock and disco in the 1970s. There are as many rock n roll aficionados who would be as condemning as I am of rap about disco and punk music.

Every generation has its own musical cross to bear. When growing up I would purchase Rolling Stone magazine or Billboard magazine, it was essential for me to own every album by every artists on the Top 100 list. Today when looking at any Top 100 list I would rather become deaf than admit I own any of what is considered good music.

Maybe this is what happens to every one due to aging. We become hard of hearing and sooner or later we can't distinguish one song from another. I doubt that. Music has charms to sooth the average beast.

BEARS

A famous author was once asked what animal best described all writers. He did not hesitate to respond immediately, he said "Bears." When asked why Bears? He said, "Hibernation." Writers have an odd reputation for being unsociable. This reputation has not changed since the first caveman began drawing on cave walls to tell a story. As the ways of expressing the written word changed with the times, writers found better ways to be unsociable. Their stories influenced by the society they lived in got more expressive until it became necessary to stop drawing stick figures on walls and write them on paper. Paper replaced rock as the most powerful method for sharing ideas, concepts and stories. According to Wikipedia which is the modern equivalent for the encyclopedia there's a game people play called Rock – Paper – Scissors. It is played between two people who form symbols representing each element. The "rock" beats scissors, the "scissors" beat paper and the "paper" beats rock; if both players throw the same shape, the game is tied. Other names for the game in the English-speaking world include roshambo, ick-ack-ock and other orderings of the three items, sometimes with "rock" being called "stone."

I would argue the point that if the pen is mightier than the sword, than in actuality paper is the strongest element in the aforementioned game. If you think about it we have heard the phrase a million times – "the contract is binding." What element do you think the contract is made of? I rest my case. The hibernation factor associated with writers is a long standing phenomenon. Every generation has their paper back heroes. For the modern generation the writers have found a genre of writing which would be considered dime store quality stories. The heroes of today's generation write about lions, tigers and bears – oh my. Actually it has more to do with wizards, witches, dragons and soothsayers capable of magic tricks. The modern generation has an appreciation for escape in the same way generations before discovered literature worthy of a higher level of intellect. It is unfair to diminish the writer's today for filling the niche created by video games and comic books. Writers write about the interests of the public at any given time. A buddy and I often spend weekends traveling the eastern seaboard in search of used book stores. These book stores are the last refuge of our past appreciation for writers. The writers we admire both fictional and non-fiction in nature had their day long ago. The place where there work is physically available has diminished as well. The large corporate box stores are nothing more than a market place for the remaining publishing companies to display their wares.

When entering a box store anywhere in America, the most ridiculous surprise awaits the book buyer. There are kiosks set up to promote devices so people can read books on them. It's similar to an executioner asking you what color rope would you like when they hang you. This metaphor may sound a tad over-the-top, but it's the sensation I get whenever entering one of these stores. In a good used book store – the sensation is the same kind I remember when books were books. You can smell a good book; it smells like you can imagine it should – like the writer burned his candles at both ends struggling to piece together his story. In the 21st century there are generations already born who have never needed to see the inside of a book store. Many kids today think their parents are writers because they see them writing on their phones and other devices all day. For that matter many kids consider themselves to be writers because they do the same thing. Writers once had a stature of nobility in the world. Many vacated the throne with the advent of the Internet. Don't get me wrong – the Internet is a marvelous thing. At its best it promotes world-wide communication and provides levels of entertainment found nowhere on the physical planet.

It is not a real world by any means. The writers of yesteryear who wrote in the context of their eras "dime store trade" predicted the society we live in today. Those visionary authors of science fiction saw it coming before any of us could have imagined. Science fiction was once labeled a lower form of writing by the same companies who embrace every star studded tale a writer could dream up.

Meanwhile, the lower form of writing today has been demoted to the bottom shelf. Stories related to growing up in a small town surrounded by eccentric characters needs to be told as if it were a memoir. There are no "To Kill a Mockingbird" or "Worlds According to Garp" authors anymore. Unless of course the author includes some hefty embellishments like sex, drugs and the occasional mass murdering terrorist.

Writers have their own place in cyberspace. There are millions of BLOG writers who some make a good living if they have enough followers. A good BLOG gets sponsors which in turn sell advertising to the members of the BLOG which generates an income for the writers. God Bless Capitalism in Cyberspace!

This all sounds rather cynical of our modern world. I would argue the truth hurts. A friend of mine when I first told him I was thinking of writing a novel said to me – "The world needs stories." I advised him the world has more stories then they know what to with today. He replied, "They don't have yours unless you write it."

In many interviews conducted throughout time with writers they inevitably are asked the question who influenced them. The writers of today have a very short list. They want to write books that have the ability of becoming movies or series on HBO. Good for them.

It leaves room for the real story tellers to keep writing.

ATLAS HUGGED

If it can be said, dreams create memories than Atlas has been hugged many times throughout history. A location in Glendale New York was named the Atlas Terminals when it was first purchased by Henry Hemmerdinger n 1922. Henry was a rag-man. It can be said, no better example of a rags to riches story exists in our world.

The original owners of the property known today as the Atlas Terminal Mall in Glendale bought fabric scraps and sold them as waste to other industries. In the early days of industry such products were necessary to assist in the manufacturing of merchandise. The visionary qualities of one family established the Atlas terminal as one of the first industrial parks in America.

Through the years many companies have rented or purchased buildings in the Atlas terminals. Railroad connections were incorporated in to the complex to assist in moving goods across the country. Some of the companies who benefited from this site are a part of our nation's history to this day:

- General Electric
- Kraft
- Westinghouse and
- NY Telephone

The Hemmerdinger family went on to become investors in many real estate ventures owning buildings in all boroughs of New York. As times changed and industry advanced with the advent of machinery and other aspects of modern technology, the lucrative business of fabric scraps became unprofitable. Many John Galt's have come and gone through the gates and byways we know as Atlas Terminal Mall today. In case you are not familiar with the name John Galt – he was a fictional character in the book Atlas Shrugged by Ayn Rand. His character is established as the ultimate dreamer. He represents the aura surrounding the entrepreneurs of the working class. There have been many dreams and lives affected by this stretch of 20 or so acres located on Cooper Avenue and Dry Harbor Road (now known as 80th Street) in Glendale, NY. The original name of the company "Atlas Waste Manufacturing Company" grew out of what were once farmland and a little mill for processing potatoes.

From this plot of land once can envision an entire community reliant on potatoes as their main source of income and livelihood. As a resident of Glendale for 50 years, I can attest to the many changes to the neighborhood, none of which can be associated with the original landscape.

By the 1950s, all or most of Glendale became residential providing homes for families who long ago embraced the American dream. Only a few homes exist today that were part of the original landscape. Through the years developers have changed the buildings and streets to house both homes and businesses along the byways that surround the community.

If pressed for definition, Glendale in keeping with the Hemmerdinger vision was the original dumping site for both industry and mankind. Glendale is home to several cemeteries which were utilized early on in the 20th century when Manhattan could no longer keep pace with its dead.

Glendale is also home to a 400 plus Acre Park. The area of land that makes up Forest Park is a trophy place for all things relevant to nature. The park according to many historians was formed by glaciers over 20,000 years go. It was at one time home to many Native American Indian tribes.

Today, the park continues to enchant its visitors with open spaces and amenities not found anywhere else. The Carousel located near the Woodhaven Boulevard entrance is one of the last remaining man-carved wooden horses and animals rides in the world.

One cannot help but wonder if one of the main hubs for industry – Atlas Terminals saw anything related to what Glendale would become in the future.

The future arrives without our noticing sometimes and nowhere is there better evidence than what the Atlas Mall became in the early part of the 21st century. Several books have been written throughout time depicting the changing landscapes of America. Many in recent years establish the fact we are a mall-centric society. We love to shop.

The website for the current location is labeled, The Shops at Atlas Mall. Included in the shops are clothing and shoe stores and several restaurants. A centerpiece of the Mall is the open-air parcel of land located in the middle of the buildings. Here too change has occurred in the brief time the Mall was established in 2006. What was once an open field surrounded by trees and a small fountain has been developed to accommodate kiosk for food establishments.

To further expound on the changes in what is a brief history, the community has witnessed several owners with different views on what the Mall should be.

When the Atlas Mall first opened it housed a different set of standards that at first were overwhelming to the community. Major clothing chains like Steinmart and Joseph A. Bank promoted their wares to what they were told was an upper middle class Glendale.

The original vision included novelty stores that sold stationary and high-end wedding items and accessories. In the mix was a supermarket called The Amish Market. This market was indeed a luxury for the community. It had a special personality that included a butcher with quality meats and a fruits and vegetables area that sold fresh goods on a daily basis.

As the first years progressed, the original investment by the owners did not warrant what they considered to be a worthy profit. Changes began to take shape in ways that made loyal customers shrug with disdain.

One of the main businesses that were part of the original plan was Borders Book and Music. The arrival of a book store that residents of Glendale and its surrounding communities like Middle Village could embrace as their own was a godsend. Never before in my memory as a resident did I see so many members of my neighborhood thoroughly alive with enthusiasm and joy.

The book store housed major events throughout its history including book signings and was part of the last great American literature phenomenon known as the Harry Potter craze. When Harry Potter books were released it became a celebration for children of all-ages. Midnight release parties were held with customers lined up inside and outside of the store.

One of my personal life-long memories will always be having had the honor of a book signing for my novel "Something in the Neighborhood of Real." The novel is about my younger days growing up in Glendale and sharing it with the community was a glorious moment.

Going in to the bookstore and seeing one's own book on the shelves is not something many can experience. It is perhaps my main reason for calling this essay – Atlas Hugged.

Every hug ends and we are left with a feeling of having had a special moment. The Atlas Mall has a history that dates back to the birth of its surrounding neighborhoods. The current owners seek to establish it as a main shopping location. Somewhere John Galt is looking down and wondering if they have the vision to embrace the neighborhoods or squeeze the residents for everything they can steal.

A.O.R.

In the late 1960s radio initiated a new format for music lovers. The FM dial was filled with stations that played Album Oriented Rock music. This A.O.R. format embraced the concept of rock music as a new art form. Up until that time music lovers heard rock music as a singles-only format on Top 40 radio stations.

The single or 45rpm was the record of choice for promoting the music of groups and singers in the rock genre. Albums until this time became the norm for record buyers or fans of Jazz and Classical music.

The ability to sit and listen to an entire record by a single group or singer was marginally practiced by listeners. This changed drastically when records called "concept albums" started to celebrate the visionary qualities of the artist making music. The records that pushed the medium over the top were Pet Sounds by the Beach Boys, which in turn as legend has it prompted the Beatles to create Sgt. Pepper's Lonely Hearts Clubs Band. The concept album was born giving way for rock bands to tell a story or embrace a certain mood over the length of a 33 1/3 rpm record.

When rock artist Beck's record "Morning Phase" was named Album of the Year in 2014 much was lost on the average music fan of today. Sadly in the modern phase of music the ability for fans to enjoy an entire album in one listening is highly suspect. What should be a progressive formula for enjoying music has been turned again in to an artist being recognized for a single song on an album.

This is due in part to the manner in which music can be purchased today on platforms like iTunes. The phrase "music lovers" has been reversed in its appreciation of music as an art form; because it is produced and marketed to create a sensation rather than a cultivated piece of musical expression. By awarding the Album of the Year award to Beck's record leaves hope for the future of music as a sustaining element of artistry. The hoopla surrounding rap singer Kanye West's indignant display of ignorance when acting in a way both unprofessional and disrespectful towards Beck further proves the depths to which the industry has fallen.

During the 2009 Grammy Music Awards Mr. West stormed the stage when record of the year was awarded to singer Taylor Swift. He performed the same gesture when the Album of the Year award was presented to Beck. In both incidents he begged artist indifference blaming the Grammy organization of not recognizing "real" talent.

What is quite disturbing is the inability for Mr. West to understand music is not defined by his standards alone. The rap or pop records without my being labeled "over the hill" by today's standards have "hits" which does not constitute them as having a lasting impression on the public.

Singles do not define a band or singers art. It is for some very difficult to understand that society has a certain level of sophistication related to the music one might choose to embrace. Again, not wishing to be labeled "over the hill" today's music "hits" lack the qualities once associated with artistry. Catchy tunes which become sing-a-long favorites for a teen based medium have very little possible chance of being considered art or ground-breaking.

The record companies today lack any visionary talents proven by the often formula driven music heard on the air waves and in clubs. The average listener who embraces these songs wishes only to keep dancing in a frenzy state not caring at all what song may be playing.

Lacking in the condemnation of Mr. West's comments blaming the Grammy organization for its inability to recognize artistry is perhaps the biggest flaw in support of good music versus bad. In no way can a good hit be denied its place in history; but in no way can it be defined as art.

Art by definition is the expression or application of human creative skill and imagination, typically in a visual form such as painting or sculpture, producing works to be appreciated primarily for their beauty or emotional power. What happens when music becomes formularized is it often predictable and void of any lasting impression.

When A.O.R. became the prime resource for music lovers, the bar so to say was lifted in defining what was good versus kitschy music. Top 40 radio again embraced its standards for playing music defined as "favorites" over a world-wide controlled listening space; while bands willing to express their artistic fervor thrived. The Who's "Tommy" and "Quadrophenia" are prime examples of this practice.

Concept albums do not make the record company's rich. Instead they allow the listening public to realize there is music being made that qualifies the medium as worthy of being an art form. Mr. West would like everyone to buy his records even if every song on the album sounds exactly the same. His concept is based on the belief his fans do not care about the music as much as they crave a beat.

WEATHER

The 21st century has proven to be a most difficult world-wide phenomenon where weather is concerned. Record breaking levels of rainfall and snow accumulation remain front page news. High temperatures in summer months and low temperatures in winter have created concern for those who share in the philosophy of global warming.

What is still debatable in most countries cannot be dismissed as mere coincidence in others. What must be included in any commentary related to these weather conditions is how they are reported.

To become a meteorologist is not an exact science. In part the study of math, science and the history of weather fall in to a wide range of study. However, most meteorologist of the television age are personalities capable of entertaining the public while forecasting the weather.

Society has taken to relying on seeing their news presented to them in a certain way. Given the wide-range of personalities associated with giving us our weather on a daily basis, much has been derived about what they look like in appearance and dress. What happens when viewers tune in for their daily dose of news has very little relevance to whether it is accurate or worthy of true facts.

More times than we can count the weather is forecast as best and worst case scenarios. The meteorologist is interpreting what they see and believe to be inclement weather. In America, the Weather Channel holds a monopoly of sorts for representing the weather around the world.

We as viewers tune in to see what is being broadcast for our area and can be privy to announcements about weather all over the world. Local stations take their weather predicting skills to new levels of audacity given the way and means their interpretation of the weather is presented.

While the subject of "weather" can be quite fascinating when looked upon as a global phenomenon that occurs every day differently all around the world; local broadcasters tend to sensationalize their moment in the "sun." The catch phrase associated with their egos being more important than the accuracy of the weather, we are prone to saying, "they don't know what they are talking about."

In many cases this is the only explanation for being found in a sudden downpour when the weatherman advised it was going to be a sunny day. The worst example of the power the weather announcers have on the human psyche is evident every winter when snowfalls are reported as tell-tale signs of the apocalypse. Full scale attacks on the safety and well-being of all in the path of a storm causes panic.

People go to supermarkets and hardware stores in record numbers seeking enough food to survive and supplies to ward off the impending doom. It never fails to astonish how we react to weather predictions. In every other aspect of our daily lives mankind remains calm or indifferent based on their opinion of a certain societal problem.

However, weather stands alone as a medium that unites us as a species lacking common sense. The expectation levels related to our individualized sense of entitlement turn some in to raving lunatics.

Despite the level of panic caused by the prediction of weather changes, no one is held accountable. If for example a financial advisor was to make predictions based on his expertise related to sales – and his predictions kept falling short of what was expected, he would be fired. If for example a teacher was to expect all his/her students be held to the same standard, they would be fired. If for example, every worker in any industry decided they could embellish the truth to make themselves appear more important, they would be found out and fired.

But, meteorologists are not held to any such standards. They can interpret the weather any way they deem newsworthy and the public has to believe them. There is no denying that weather related changes in the atmosphere are drastically evolving in to a major concern for people. What constitutes concern cannot be compared to our gullible nature,

A most recent prediction of a storm to end all storms in New York caused schools to be closed, businesses to close, motorist advised to stay off public roads and the closing of the subway system for the first time in its history. What was most evident during this panic that never amounted to the severity being predicted was not the inability of meteorologist but more so admittance by officials they can no longer guarantee our safety. Government officials like local weather personalities are entertainers prone to concerns about their reputations. By over-reacting they prevent the calamities associated with handling natural disasters. Hurricane Katrina in Louisiana and the Gulf states as well as Hurricane Sandy in the North East states have become iconic for the level of damage made possible by the weather. The government can no longer afford to assist the average citizen in the event of a weather related catastrophe.

The domino effect of how bad any storm might be causes the public to react with seeking supplies and the government to over react throwing everything they got to avoid disaster.

This does not stop local officials from declaring their cities and towns disaster areas. The reason being everything is based on hearsay and preparing for such incidents requires a crystal ball not a specialized weather station.

Whether you believe the changes in weather are a result of man-made ignorance or merely a new phase in the planets evolution, we can no longer consider weather as a form of entertainment. The smiling weatherman or the skimpy clad female meteorologist cannot be taken seriously.

They in turn cannot be the determining factor in proving our officials are inept in supporting any ability to prepare properly for any natural disaster. What comes to the surface with regard to what nature can do, is there any hope in securing our safety given what mankind can do to harm us? The 21st century has made us all aware how vulnerable we are to nature and those around us.

THE DECLINE OF LITERATURE

The decline of literature has been a swan song for every generation of writers and readers alike since the advent of the Internet. Every one capable of using a keyboard can label themselves as writers open to everyone as reading material. In as much as the highbrow statement suggests the decline as a medium, it is also important to realize the actual content of our recent best sellers warrant serious investigation.

The Internet killed the book stores in the same way it was proposed Video Killed the Radio Star back when MTV was all about music. However, here too we are losing sight of the origins of literature as opposed to where good literature might be available.

Putting aside the obvious for a moment as more and more book stores close around the world, the actual availability of a good story written by a voice for any generation is forever lost. I realize this is a blatant statement with total disregard for the books released today. I can assure you the reader there are authors capable of writing a book for our times, however if the author does not fit in to the formula driven criteria for books published, you will more than likely need to look at the thousands of books self- published each month.

The formula in place for publishers today requires every book have a cross marketing capability. This translates to a book being marketed to the movie industry as well as having a niche marketing capability in the fashion world as well.

To further elaborate on this dissertation of the modern literary community we need go no further than the last great world-wide phenomenon in writing: The Harry Potter Factor. What J.K. Rowling's wizard world books did for the industry and to literature in general has diminished the ability for future generations to learn anything about era driven literature.

Witnessing the reaction of young readers who consumed Harry Potter books like peanut butter and jelly sandwiches at a lunch time picnic; the publishing companies tossed out any regiment for discovering new authors. Instead the onus is now more in keeping with discovering a new phenomenon.

In quick succession the formula can be discovered in the popularity of series driven books like The Hunger Games, Twilight Series of Books and as of this writing, the latest phenomenon Fifty Shades of Gray. These books generate an interest for female oriented literary heroes and heroines.

Without stepping in to a trap by condemning or applauding these new literary sensations, suffice to say literature given these books as example has become trendy and cannot or will not be hailed as worthy of anyone's must read books for a school assignment. In two prior essays in this collection – Writing and Bears I mention the value of writing as a form of cultivated art form. What the popularity of these books says about our culture begs for definition.

Despite what may be labeled my misunderstanding of these literary phenomenon's, I again must digress by advising you the reader the intellectual stimulation once discovered by past generations is at serious risk of losing any comparative values. The mention of these highly successfully cross marketed books only skims to the surface of what may be defined as literature today. I will not discuss the male oriented fascination with books about war, espionage and International Financial coups. Nor will I venture in to the world of lawyers as heroes fighting against the rights and wrongs of small town America or world events related to global warming. Suffice to say our male readers want to believe they are well informed about worldly events based on the type of characters they embrace as superheroes.

This essay is driven not by disdain for the aforementioned literary assassinations, but by a newly devised medium labeled, the Autobiographical Novel.

The Internet (or the heir apparent to defining everything and everything – Wikipedia defines this kind of book as follows:) An autobiographical novel is a form of novel using Autofiction techniques, or the merging of autobiographical and fictive elements. The literary technique is distinguished from an autobiography or memoir by the stipulation of being fiction. Because an autobiographical novel is partially fiction, the author does not ask the reader to expect the text to fulfill the "autobiographical pact".

Let's dissect this definition shall we?

Autofiction? If you type the word in to your Microsoft Word application on your computer it is not recognized as a word. Does the word sensationalism come to mind? The narrative for this kind of book has no basis in literary format. It can abide by its own code of ethics related to anything the author wishes to convey about his life at any given time during the story. Key word in the sentence above is "story", it is a contrived formula for making the author appear more real than he or she may be.

The literary technique as defined falls in to its own spectrum of realism. This is akin to our current fascination with reality television. Scripted reality has no basis for being something that can happen or did happen. Reality television, like any book purported to be of this new form, Autobiographical Novel, is a forced criterion for selling stories under a new literary marquee.

If I may indulge you the reader further, the A.N. is like someone releasing their diary and adding elements to make their life more interesting. For example an entry in someone's diary may say: I hate my job and all the people I work for. In the A.N. the sentence becomes - I hate my job so I plotted to make a statement which would change the world forever.

The A.N. is an embellishment of the truth to enhance the reader's interest. The latest world-wide fascination with one writer's Autobiographical Novel is from Norway. Karl Ove Knausgård has written six volumes under this auspicious category. In his own home country he is considered a literary giant. His gut wrenching truisms related to his struggles throughout his life is being called by some a modern day Marcel Proust.

Nevertheless, let us not get too bogged down in the type of things people write or read. The accepted phrase by most individuals is at least people are reading. I would agree if there were any stories that did not capture a falsified category of embellished truth or fall in to Publishing Industry formula driven standards for what is considered literature.

We must again assimilate the title of this book of essays, rants and monologues to best define what is happening to our society. People can live vicariously through the heroes of far off worlds in dangerous circumstances or they can be excited by books that formulate sexual situations that belittle their daily unhappy lives.

Once upon a time several writers fell in to the category of "guilty pleasure". Those writers at least had a penchant for creating real life situations with characters derived from everyday life. The recommendation I highly share with anyone who values their own intelligence is to visit a used book when wishing to discover good writing. The modern equivalent has taken to creating stories that provide gratuitous sex and violence as shock value.

HOW TO TRAIN YOUR PET ROCK

In 1975 in the state of California, in the county of Santa Cruz, in a town named Bonny Doon, Gary Dahl got the idea for a trend that lasted less than one year, but netted him enough money to become a millionaire. Dahl after listening to his friends complaints about their pets came up with the idea to market rocks as pets. It took off as a massive marketing campaign displaying rocks packaged in customized boxes with an instruction booklet on how to take care of your pet rock.

In the same burst of modern day ingenuity using the "pet rock" as a metaphor for our daily obsessions, I now present instructions for training your pet rock.

We all have them today in different forms. One person's pet rock can be their cell phone. They are so attached to their pet rock they cannot help but check on it every five to ten minutes. This leads to a higher level of attention deficit disorder (ADD) than ever recorded before in the history of mankind. Phone obsession includes a need to dress your phones to look a certain way. Like the pet rock phenomenon which was immediately known to be a huge trendy play on words, today's phone obsessives cannot help but rely on objects as if they were an extension of their personality.

The pet rock phone lovers need to embrace some simple methods for separating them from this addiction.

(1) It's not real. It does not contain the meaning of life and death. The stored information inside the phone will not make you in to a better human being.

(2) It does not require nurturing. The phone does not rely upon you to take care of it. It runs on a battery. If the battery runs low it does not mean you have a terminally ill friend.

(3) It cannot speak or help you. The devices that have convinced you every phone has its own unique personality are a ploy. Your phone will not automatically know when you need to hear from someone. You cannot have a conversation with it without someone else or some computerized device being involved.

(4) Your fingers will not fall off if you do not send a text every 10 minutes. You are not as important nor is the information sent by your friends as important as you think.

(5) When you plug it in at night, you are not tucking in a child.

(6) If your phone dies, it does not mean you need to arrange for a funeral.

(7) You do not need to dress so you match your phone's appearance.

(8) Your pet rock is not better looking or more intelligent than someone else's. They all come with different features and space limitations. You made the choice to own your phone, it did not choose you.

(9) Your pet rock lacks the ability to turn you in to a super hero.

(10) You alone are responsible for everything stored on your phone; it does not have ability to plot against you.

Another pet rock for our modern society is the ownership of a car. Cars are marketed with an air of making the driver feel cool. The only feature necessary for ownership of any car is:

(1) Whether it will get you to your destination and back.

(2) Provide you and your family with safety.

(3) It does not require comforts equivalent to your living room.

(4) It is not a fashion statement you can wear like designer clothing.

(5) All cars are subject to conditions beyond their capabilities. The state of the road and the elements due to weather do not suddenly make your car safer to drive than another. You as the driver control your own destiny.

(6) There is no such thing as driving in complete silence, this is a myth created by car manufacturers to make you think style and luxuries guarantee you comforts found only in the vast vacuum of outer space.

(7) How many times a week you need to wash your car does not make it perform better.

(8) Bigger cars do not make up for your lack of happiness in the bedroom.

(9) Female drivers are not worse drivers than male drivers. They may multi-task more while driving which creates this illusion, but the actual better than or worse than simulation is purely incidental.

(10) Most cars boast of reaching certain speeds in less than 60 seconds. It is important to understand most speeds they can reach are not suitable for city driving. Also speed is not an option anyone needs to look for when buying a car. You will get to where you are going based on traffic and the number of detours you will inevitably face every day.

The training of our pet rocks in the modern world comes with great patience. Very few individuals are content to exist without their added conveniences. Our sense of entitlement has created an aura around us which is suitable to those individuals suffering from delusions. A glorious example of our modern day pet rock associations comes in the form of how we choose to spend our time.

The oldest inherited pet rock from our forefathers is the television we own. No longer are people content to own a television, they have to have an entertainment system suitable for viewing everything as if it were being shown in a major motion picture theatre. Here too the pet rock phenomenon requires serious training:

(1) The size of your screen does not make what you are watching better. The movie or show is good or bad based on its content not on how it is viewed. This stipulation is open to debate given an extension of this pet rock obsession prone to special effects.

(2) The sound system of your television does not need to be the equivalent to a live music extravaganza.

(3) The latest craze experienced by many viewers has its own catch phrase: Binge watching. This pet rock trait enables viewers to watch entire seasons of a series in one sitting. The result of this kind of viewing enables us to become part of the show we are watching. No longer are we watching a show, we are a character sitting in the corner of the room or living next door to everyone in the show.

(4) Every family needs only one television. The number of television shows will always outnumber the number of TV's we can own.

(5) Reality television is not real. The cameraman is not following real people, he is following real scripted situations.

(6) You are not what you watch. What you watch gets made popular because you watch it.

(7) The television was dubbed the "boob tube" shortly after it became popular based on its ability to take the place of human interaction in our living rooms. Today with televised capabilities on devices in our cars and on our wrists we are quickly becoming a society of boobs no matter where we go or what we do.

(8) No news media station or service has a bird's eye view of any situation. They boast of providing the viewer with exclusive takes on events because no two news reporters are alike. This may be the only true fact associated with knowing your pet rock television has any chance of providing you with an experience no one else has.

(9) You cannot as yet surgically attach a remote to your hand. Although given our penchant for holding on to our devices this actuality may be difficult to prove.

(10) As an aside anyone who says they don't watch television or at worse say they don't own a television is

(1) Homeless or

(2) A liar.

Exceptions to this rule can be found in third world countries where water is more precious than gold or the leaders of a country are terrified what the content may do to their citizens. The leaders in these countries are labeled oppressors, while in many respects they may be the last great protectors of human integrity.

Pet rocks are everywhere we turn. These short study mentions are about the obvious modern day attachments we are convinced we cannot live without.

On the highest mountains or the depths of our oceans we now have pet rocks that assist the traveler in getting to the top faster or across the great divides safer.

The Pet rock for travelers today is the GPS. This voice generated mapping system guides us everywhere we want to go. Had it been around during the voyage of the Titanic we would have avoided tragedy at sea. Had it been available during climbs of Everest we would have avoided deaths on land. Had it been available as a resource during flights we would have avoided loss of life in the air.

However, the GPS makes one aspect of the American Dream a lost entity. We can no longer travel as true adventurers lost to the outside world. We can no longer rely on our instincts to guide us during unknown circumstances.

Of course one might argue we can simply choose to travel without a GPS device. Maybe we choose to avoid this kind of adventure because many already realize how truly lost we already might be before we walk out our front door.

STRUGGLING WITH REALITY

What has been wrought by the popularity of Karl Ove Knausgaard? The embrace of his work as a literary sensation leaves little room for normal criticism. While the literary world falls head over heels for his observation tangent-like musings every man, woman and child should quietly begin compiling every note, card, and letter ever received and ready it for publication.

   In case you dear reader have missed out on the current phenomenon of Mr. Knausgaard's work, I will attempt a brief description. He hails from Norway and has won every conceivable literary award for his writing. What kind of writer is he you might ask? He writes about everything and everyone in a way that has him being compared to Marcel Proust. Now then, if your intellect serves you well, you may consider such a comparison worthy of celebration. I dare ask the average reader, have you read Proust? The conundrum when asked such a question in our modern world leaves the average person in hysterics. It is after all not necessary to read Proust, the mere mention of his name and therefore anyone being compared to him creates awe.

Recently Mr. Knausgaard was commissioned to write an article for the NY Times magazine. This magazine is as of this writing going through a massive rebirth attempting to make it more literally relevant in a world forecasting the end of printed books. His assignment is something of a dream job for any writer of his caliber. He was asked to write a travelogue memoir about the sights and sounds of the America long forgotten in modern literary circles. Should the NY Times be so obviously accommodating to a foreign writer when asking him to write about visiting America? A letter should be sent immediately by any writer with a penchant for travel to the Norwegian consulate requesting an assignment to visit Norway and write about the sights and sounds from an American perspective. Of course this would not prove beneficial to anyone, especially when Norway requires a writer capable of recognizing writing as an art form. Unless of course, there is by chance a new kind of writing that caters to the Facebook reading audience. Then again, in Mr. Knausgaard's defense his musings would be scrolled past by so many members of the Facebook population, the earth may be in danger of falling off its imaginary axis. Why you may ask is one writer upset by the success of another? It sounds like jealousy but in actuality it is a cry for justice. What size is the actual audience for books that average 400 plus pages and take the reader through a myriad of musings on simple day to day experiences? In the first of two articles written for the NY Times, our modern day Marcel Proust contemplates for nearly an entire page about the indignity of asking the front desk at the hotel he is staying at for a plunger when his toilet overflows. This is high end stimuli for the new intellectual publishing community.

  What we are witnessing is a ways and means to make relevant the daily simplistic activities of life as we know it. Where most writers would be condemned for taking 500 words to say what a good editor will cut down to one paragraph, Mr. Knausgaard is being hailed as genius. The contents of these "autobiographical novels" consume the reader with a new form of literary escape. The Internet has brought forth a new need for readers, the ability to feel like voyeurs even when we read what others say and do on a daily basis. The format for such renderings provide the kind of escape once appreciated when reading books about traveling through deserts or lost on mountains. A new kind of intrigue is opened up to the reader who can live vicariously through the life time memories of another person's conquest, hopes, fears and sexual practices.

Anyone struggling with their own reality can live someone else's life leaving behind their own trials and tribulations. What the swan song publishing companies are doing is an insult to the integrity of real readers around the world. The men and women manning the decks for publishing companies are no longer looking for writers; they are searching for phenomenon. If any of these rants sound familiar I touched upon the Knausgaard phenomenon briefly in a prior essay. However given the subject matter, it is insulting to Mr. Knausgaard to limit such commentary to brief mention.

Since the average writer of modern America knows well he has a very small and limited audience, I can embellish this commentary in any shape form and fashion I deem interesting. Take for example the style of writing being embraced by the awards given to our new Marcel Proust? Let me try writing something in his style based on what I was doing during the writing of this essay. I could share my own autobiographical musing given a fictional flare for the readers' amusement.

Living as I do in New York, at a period in history when technology rules my waking hours I can start by advising you the writer that it has been unseasonably cold this winter. How cold was it you might ask? It's been so cold that mention of snow in the Northeast is the equivalent of telling people we are under attack by space aliens. Given this fact more people have contemplated moving to warmer climates than ever before in the history of our country. However, New Yorkers are by nature a stubborn breed and mere climatic torture does not constitute reason for surrender. We are after all aware that according to Wallace Shawn and Andre Gregory people talk about leaving New York all the time. In a movie entitled "My Dinner with Andre", which by and large may well be the first movie privy to the phrase autobiographical fiction both characters sit for two hours in a restaurant discussing what can be deemed as the meaning of life. The average movie goer if told to sit and watch this film would contemplate suicide. The viewer is asked to witness a dinner conversation that takes us on a roller coaster ride of emotions, thoughts and ideas. During the aforementioned commentary about leaving New York Andre Gregory announces that people who live in New York are the builders of the new concentration camp. As inhabitants New Yorkers are so proud of the concentration camp they call home they cannot leave it.

What this type of writing proves is the average reader will undoubtedly skip over paragraphs if not entire pages to discover if a point is being made by the writer. Given the curious nature of fans of Mr. Knausgaard's we can only assume they have become masters of tolerating such musings or in effect experts at realizing much of what is being shared has no basis of pushing the story forward. Instead the books are void of plot and based on taking the reader anywhere the writer feels like going.

Here is the caveat for such reading, which may after all my sorted baiting above surprise you. It is refreshing. It is glorious on par with the great works of fiction from the likes of Tolstoy, Dickens and yes Marcel Proust himself. In such masterpieces of literature the stories seem stagnated at times because we as the reader cannot fathom such simplicity necessary to telling the stories. Is it relevant in War and Peace to define every name as if we ourselves were members on the family tree? To read such work takes patience and commitment which in comparison to most books written today filled with "a page turning frenzy plot" about what building or train or plane is about to be blown up; does in fact represent a pleasant alternative.

The popularity of American writing has become nonexistent in part because the publishing industry has no eyes and ears open to new trends in writing. It took a scrappy Norwegian writer sharing his memoirs with a knack for embellishing the truth to make the world aware every writer does not have to create a serial killer to gain recognition. It took Mr. Knausgaard's six volumes under the guise of "My Struggle" to show us stories about everyday living is as important as chasing spies across Europe or in to the Congo.

Nevertheless, there is something to be said about my wanting to travel to Norway. I am now quite curious about their sewer systems and whether they can handle my diet.

BANNED TO SIBERIA

The first time I read the word "Siberia" was in a book by Aleksandr Solzhenitsyn, The Gulag Archipelago. I had never heard of the author or knew anything about Russian prison camps. The discovery of this other world where people were sent in many cases to die intrigued me. As a young man the reality of such a place was better than any science fiction plot I may have read. I continued pursuing Solzhenitsyn's exploits in his novels and subsequent works related to stories involving his exile. He was in a strange way deported by the government to of all places Vermont in America. I could not fathom how being deported to anywhere in America could be considered a punishment. He lived in Vermont for 17 years. This is not a story about him but more so about the concept of Siberia. It may be said many people live in their own private Siberia. I would agree with this possibility given the way our modern world inadvertently causes people to assume isolation through a personality they present on social media. I came early to the social media phenomenon when AOL was one of the only games in town. I call it a game because the experience of using AOL chat rooms and membership to exclusive online groups was very entertaining. The experiences I had introduced me to people who had one thing in common - we all listened to the same radio show: Vin Scelsa's Idiots Delight.

The radio show introduced me to music I would have never been exposed to. Also, Vin Scelsa in many ways was a voice on the radio that became the only source of music and literary intelligence for me growing up. When the membership to a group called the Idiots Delight Digest presented itself I leaped at the opportunity to become a member. Embracing the shows introductory premise repeated at the beginning of every show:

Respect The Elders.

Embrace The New.

Encourage the Impractical and Improbable, Without Bias

David Fricke

What transpired for me personally after joining the group in 1995 when the Internet was beginning its prominent status we know today; offered insights in to how social media works. Throughout the infancy of online chat groups people inevitably come to a point of realizing it is not a very nice place to visit. Maybe the word "visit" is a tad overzealous, you can visit the Internet sites without being bothered, but if you join groups of any kind, you will learn fast it is more about ownership than acceptance of opinion. FACEBOOK is the current mainstay social media haven for groups supporting any and all things interesting to people. What starts out as "place" to get information and share your opinion inevitably will and most terms turn ugly. It may be evidence of human nature that one person's opinion on any issue will quickly be met with condemnation. How this happens requires stepping away from the melee for a period of time. Hence, excommunication is the only resource for maintaining one's ultimate sanity. When each Vin Scelsa's show promotes his opening statement as quoted above by David Fricke it offers the listener a comforting premise, whereby listeners are going to be entertained by the deejay using songs as his metaphoric journey. This served me well for close to 30 years before being introduced to other people who enjoyed the same show. While it was a joyful celebration of sorts, finally realizing I was not alone in my appreciation of the show – the overall experience proved challenging. What the show's members represented once they had a forum on line to voice their personal experiences and opinion became a study in human ambivalence at times. Because it was a small group of some 500 members the experience still represents a magical example of discovering there are individuals inspired and influenced in the same ways. However, the diversity of any forum soon raises it nasty head when politics, religion and social status enter the equation. For the most part using this very early example of combined communications between a formative groups of people serves as a precursor to how and why people cannot for the most part exists in their own Siberian exile. At first the members who posted on a daily basis were respectful of one another. Within a span of six months via the type of things members posted or showed support for an unconscious categorization became evident. Where the original intent was to celebrate for the first time an appreciation for a radio show many had listened to for decades; over time the borders were made. A person's dislike about a certain artist Scelsa may have played on his show was met with name calling and a barrage of insults many may not have experienced since leaving High School. In many ways the experience was like a cafeteria setting where groups sat with groups and those unwelcomed in to the fray were scorned. Scelsa to his credit stayed clear of the digest politics and from time to time quoted something posted on the digest as a means of expressing his approval. For those not familiar with Vin Scelsa, he represents for music fans in New York and the surrounding states able to get the signal of the station he broadcasted from – one of the truly genuine and innovative deejays on American radio. All in all before learning there were more like myself who enjoyed his show, again I have to emphasize it was a joyful celebration. Several things have to be discussed when hailing a radio show as a means of influencing and inspiring taste; first and foremost radio listening when not used as background fodder in a restaurant or shopping mall is a private experience. Before the advent of choices when commuting in our cars, radio was our means of company during long drives. Again each listening experience was a form of escape while also being a means of imprisoned in a car waiting for traffic to lighten up. When listened to as a form of entertainment at home, a vast majority of people hear only what they want to hear and dismiss the deejay's announcements as mere commercialized interruption. This was not the case for me when listening to Scelsa. Instead I respected he was going to inform me during each show about something I did not know.

His show was in a ways a Music Education Class not given at any college. However, this is not an essay about Scelsa or his radio show. I am sharing the experience of joining an on line group who all in the beginning stages paid homage to our enjoyment for the show. Using the forum I still belong to this day, I can say many times there were incidents which caused widespread disagreements. How these arguments ensued was many times childlike in nature. It was akin to growing up and someone would yell in the schoolyard – *Your Mother Wears Combat Boots! Or – I will rank you out so low you'll think the curb is the Great Wall of China!* You have to love old insults – they were so amusing. Online, the insults almost always occurred because the person making the insult made an assumption purely on the grounds of something he / she read in a person's post. What this represented was in many ways the first sign as computer users that personality and diversity could be represented without visual or personal knowledge of another person. As a species we had somehow evolved to a level of interpreting who and what a person was simply by something they typed on a screen. A red flag went up many times during this experience whereby it was possible anyone could be **Banned to Siberia** if they did not fully embrace the popular opinion of other members.

New members to the group were welcomed with open arms – as in shouts of posts saying happy you like Vin's show! Still it has to be mentioned that there was an obvious agenda which was not created, proposed, or planned about the forum itself. The agenda had more to do with those who posted their opinions compared with the 80% who were members without a face or noticeable profile. Because it was a music appreciation group many of the members who never bothered to post during the year would surface at years end to share their Top Ten favorite albums or songs. Except for a few exceptions many of the albums and songs were represented by things Scelsa's show had introduced us to. A funny thing happened when Scelsa chose to read live on his show a post I wrote entitled "As If Elvis." Suddenly, I was singled out by our Radio God causing a ripple effect of recognition for myself and the digest as an entity Scelsa actually read. What I experienced personally as a result of this recognition was an interesting example related to human nature. Many of the members embraced the experience as being wonderful to hear something read on the air from the digest. Still, another group of individuals sent me email messages advising otherwise. What was as a prose poem written in story like fashion created a range of emotions filled with elation and condemnation. I took it all in stride and continued to post my views and opinions. Slowly, the digest became more about individual opinion then about appreciation for Scelsa's shows. Slowly, less and less information was shared about a new act he may have played or a book he was enthusiastic about. What became evident in some way was despite the fact that we all belonged to the same group to celebrate music; we were all alone in how we were allowed to say what we wanted to. I gained much to my amusement a reputation of sorts, whereby what others could say in two lines or less, I wrote full paragraphs complete with tangents and anecdotes. This was deemed unacceptable on many occasions when members felt I was taking up bandwidth on the Internet or too much space on their hard drives. What this represents in the grand scheme of modern social media circles is the awareness that less is more. People have become less inclined to read anything that they immediately determine too long for their perusal. Reading in many respects has become a limited exercise in patience. Because of our exposure to information on our devices and the groups we belong to, our allotted time for understanding another person's views or opinion is suspect. *SAY IT DON'T SPRAY IT!* Anything shared over an expected number of words is akin to spitting in the wind. It comes right back on you having never been fully expressed or it is lost without ever having been read at all. Given that despite all these personal observations the digest still thrives 20 years after its creation is a credit to the members who consider it a celebration of shared interests. The number of posts today may include one a week down from the nearly two to three dozen in its heyday. Every aspect of social media has its high and low interest group. FACEBOOK which is the current forum for all things of human interest is still in its infancy with regard to how long before members turn on one another. Already on civic association pages people are displaying their angst regarding issues like parking, common courtesy and things related to being good neighbors. Being Banned to Siberia happens every day on these pages in cyberspace where inevitably the creator of the page needs to make decisions as to what is and is not acceptable for its members. Why any creator would chose to play the role of censor is another aspect of how sensitive we are as a society when it deals with too many diverse subjects and opinions. Bans of comments by some members are warranted when it becomes quite obvious these kind of individuals enjoy shaking things up. The topic of Cyber-Bullying has become a universal problem because the same person who needs to exhibit their muscle in a schoolyard will attempt to demean others using what he / she deems as amusing on the Internet. A discussion arises whereby future generations (as in the next) will have to take classes on Cyber Etiquette. It is very easy to hurt another person's feelings with words. That old cliché many grew up hearing: "Sticks and stones will break my bones, but names will never hurt me," no longer applies. More and more people, young and old are learning the hard way the harsh ways words on a screen can cause harm. Not enough attention is being displayed for this very serious problem. More people than we care to believe are feeling they are being banned to Siberia by their peers. The next generation which I predict will turn Internet-ready in less than a decade is not adequately prepared for the evil that lurks out in Cyberspace. Whether the experience is personal or universal much of what the advances in technology have given us can be weighed on different playing fields.

Of all these fields, nowhere has there been sufficient support for how it affects people emotionally. Siberia is a lonely cold place and without proper guidance most people who visit can freeze to death and not be found until months later.

CYNICISM AND MOCKINGBIRDS

Much has been discussed about the new book, "Go Set a Watchman," by Harper Lee. Ms. Lee is best known for having written "To Kill A Mockingbird" which became a bestseller and motion picture embraced the world over as a masterpiece of literature. Now nearly 50 years later, a new book said to be written before Mockingbird is to be published. Several arguments surround the authenticity of her first books author no less to suddenly discover another existed after all this time. Long time critics of Ms. Lee's choice to be a reclusive spinster living in a small town with her sister in Alabama claimed the book was the work of her one time neighbor, Truman Capote. Capote went on to world-wide fame as an author and socialite figure in New York. He is depicted in Lee's novel as a refined but delicate soul "Dill" who visits the town where Mockingbird takes place. For many, the book To Kill a Mockingbird was a forerunner of the civil rights movement in the 1960s, giving steam to the issues related to racism in America. The book has gone on to become a staple for every school's reading list. The thought of a manuscript sitting lost and collecting dust addressing these very same issues leaves room for being skeptical about Ms. Lee as an author and the book having any real credibility when stacked up against its predecessor. Given that "Go Set a Watchman" supposedly happens after To Kill a Mockingbird we immediately have to wonder if the original publishers knew of its existence and put the cart in front of the horse. Rumors are rampant about Lee having written Go Set A Watchman first and the publisher suggesting she write a book entirely from the narrator's perspective. The narrator in Mockingbird is the daughter, Scout of Atticus Finch who tells the story of a poor black farmhand forced in to a town dispute. Further investigation reveals there was an actual real occurrence of injustice related to Ms. Lee's small town in Alabama. Lee's father was an attorney who defended a black man against racial injustice. It does not matter how Ms. Lee came to write Mockingbird, what is suspect is the appearance of a new book 50 years later that depicts the same characters. There appears to be too many questions that will forever be unanswered given Ms. Lee now in her 80s has mastered the abilities necessary for being a recluse. In my defense of Ms. Lee's right to her privacy I must question the validity of a new books appearance 50 years after the popularity of her first and only book. Writers write and unless we can be convinced she chose to write behind closed doors all these years, the stories about her being a writer spin forever in the wind. Of course I want nothing more than to believe the new book can live up to the legendary quality of Mockingbird, but I remain on the fence about it. Something may have been left in that tree trunk by Boo Radley we may never get to see. His simple mindedness may be the one behind a hoax that will mystify fans of literature for all time. Nevertheless, since todays average reader unless forced to read certain books; the voice of innocence found in Scout's observations will forever be lost as well. Her wit and wisdom while witnessing the cruelty of racism at the hands of ignorant men will only be muddled once shared from this new books perspective. Perhaps, the publishers are thrilled to have a sure best seller on their hands. Harper Lee after years of silence is being heard to say she is thrilled the book was found. Sorry Ms. Lee I won't buy it. If you could not be thrilled to publicly stand in front of a classroom in cities and towns where racism still rises it ugly head for the past 50 years, I cannot fathom you are thrilled to see anything new of yours published now or after your death. It's a hoax and again we can choose to get on the bus or walk the long road to obscurity. If this sounds too harsh, I cannot help but be angered by the entire circus surrounding a new book who has publicly avoided interviews or involvement in her own town to promote their famous neighbor. The bitterness is not mine as it seems displayed here, but a reminder to Ms. Lee you cannot have it both ways. You cannot refuse to recognize your contribution to society by declaring yourself a recluse your entire life and then tout gleeful smiles when a "lost" manuscript is discovered after all these years. Are we to believe you are a classic hoarder and the manuscript was buried under thousands of other manuscripts you started and discarded? The bitterness you displayed for 50 years is in direct conflict with the characters you supposedly created in Mockingbird. The worst cynicism I have heard surrounding the discovery of the new book comes from individuals suggesting Lee at 88 and reportedly suffering from signs of Alzheimer's could be convinced she wrote the Declaration of Independence no less the sequel or prequel to her own book. It doesn't make sense to argue over something we will never have a final answer to. Suffice to say the book will be released to the masses and be carried on to beaches comes the summer in physical and digital formats. It will become undoubtedly a major motion picture touting the favorite two subjects of Hollywood fodder these days, racism and feminism. It will cause a sensation but sadly little will change because after all it is just a book and with no one to willingly stand behind its message, again we fall victim to the ignorance of society. Now had Ms. Lee wrote her book from the perspective of Boo Radley – we may have a chance to shed light on our real problems.

ISIS IS A SONG

What is all this fuss about ISIS? The DESIRE album by Bob Dylan is over 40 years old. How could a song nearly 40 years old become so important all these years later? I mean let's be honest the average life of a song unless it was by the really BIG bands or singers like Elvis or The Beatles or The Rolling Stones just don't have a shot at being front page news no less house hold names. Ok well yeah Bob Dylan belongs on the list but ISIS? It was at best a mediocre Dylanesque kind of off shoot love song. There was this one track on the album called *"Hurricane"* which alright might be considered controversial about this boxer Ruben "Hurricane" Carter who was sent to jail for a triple murder in 1966. Turns out he did not get a fair trial and eventually was released in 1985. But ISIS, it may have made a ripple for Dylan fans but hardly the amount of splash happening today with ISIS all over the newspapers and on the nightly news. I do not really understand all the hype about this song. Briefly it's another in a long line of songs by Bob that have ulterior motives and a hidden story based on love and loyalty. It includes a quest where the guy singing the song, who I swore was Bob all these years discovers the entire thing was a folly. I don't even want to attempt sharing the lyrics with you because the song kind of freaks me out. I mean of all songs on the album how could the world be talking about ISIS like it was some major life changing song that deserves all this present day hoopla. Can we be serious for a moment and tell me why the papers and nightly news guys are not talking about *Mozambique*? It's a fun song about words that rhyme but again Bob being Bob it has a nice beat you can almost dance to. There are not many Dylan songs your average person might be willing to dance to. There are a lot of people with hang-ups in the world. I mean with all the hoopla these days about coffee shops how come no one mentions the song *One More Cup of Coffee*? It talks about gypsies and Daddy's being outlaws. You could really make a better front page story about this kind of stuff instead of ISIS! The world is really confusing if you ask me. Ok, there is other song on the album called *Oh Sister* where Bob pleads about how fragile love can be. He invokes God for the first time in assisting him to find answers. It doesn't make sense that ISIS is given so much attention since it was hardly the stand out song on the record. I mean all these video interpretations that use these violent looking dudes under the flag of ISIS wearing black masks – I don't think the producers of these videos are getting the whole Bob Dylan thing at all. And if you want to talk about Epic Dylan material there's this like 11 minute song called *Joey* which is like a novel set to music. It has all kinds of folk heroes on both sides of the spectrum. If you really want to get violent this song has it all paying homage to some mafia guy getting killed in a Clam House in Little Italy. Is there some kind of petition we can sign about how songs get misunderstood in our modern world? How about the mandolin on the song *Romance in Durango?* Another outlaw song, this time from Mexico and Bob sings in Spanish too! It could be a song used in the closing credits for an old western. This one has lyrics about shooting someone down and shots ringing out across the small mountain village. These people who report about things drive me crazy. ISIS does not deserve all the attention it is getting. I mean taken out of context the song has no value. Take for example the next song on the album – another Dylan story song called *Black Diamond Bay* about destruction and mayhem on a small island. Bob is very literary you know and this one takes its story after he read some book by Joseph Conrad. If anyone bothered to check Conrad wrote the book Heart of Darkness which was made in to a film called Apocalypse Now. That was a better excuse for all this nonsense about a song called ISIS. The album closes with a love song to his ex-wife *Sara.* The song Sara like ISIS is about marriage. Why would all this hoopla be happening about marriage? Does this have anything to do with Hollywood couples? Those people don't know how to stay married and let's face it who can blame them? Doing scenes in today's movies are so steamy there's no way they can be acting. Just imagine after making a movie with all those scenes and having to go back to some routine husband / wife lifestyle? That has to be it ISIS is being used as an acronym for marriage isn't it? What could it be? Let's figure this out together. Well since these Hollywood people spend their vacations in really hot exotic places it could be *I SUCK IN SUMMER*. Think about it, there they are with half naked people running on beaches and jumping in pools and well chances are they just go ISIS! I don't quite get the beheading references but then again, oh you have got to be kidding me! Seriously! I mean I heard of wives going ballistic but to bite something off – that's just wrong. They all walk away from the marriages loaded so why leave a guy without his manhood! This is pretty cutting edge stuff how the media gets involved in people's marriages isn't it? Maybe I have this all wrong and should do more digging on what it means. Maybe I need to get myself better informed? There was this one guy pleading we should take the threat of ISIS serious or else. What the hell does that mean? I spent hours reading the lyrics and there's mention of diamonds, pyramids and about fears of things being contagious. Perhaps I should see if Bob was in to hiding things like the Beatles if you play some of their songs backwards. Anyway, I stand by my first impression, ISIS is just a song.

BINGING

Binging once represented a person's knack for drinking too much. They went out on an all-night binge losing track of time and ending up drunk and the next morning hung over. Today the word "binging" more times than any has to do with how we watch television shows. No longer are we limited to what is presented on nightly channels, we can choose to watch entire seasons at our own leisure on NETFLIX – HULU and premium channels on cable. What this creates is widespread over saturation in our brains. The plight of a Walter White in Breaking Bad which lasted multiple seasons taking several years to view when on broadcast television can now be watched in a single weekend. By the weekend's end the viewer is in part hung over and in a manner of speaking punch drunk from having witnessed in 72 hours what it took the original viewers several years to experience. Binge watching incorporates a new form of escape for the masses, whereby we can sit in the comfort of our home power watching whatever we like when we like. There has been no official analysis done by any psychological foundation, but one can only guess how this can play in to our ever increasing mindset about entitlement.

Our sense of entitlement has already been escalated due to our want for connectivity at all times to the World Wide Web. To be separated from the luxury of checking messages, looking up information and tabulating our status updates on social media applications; we overdose on technology more times than we care to admit. Restaurants, the New York City Transit and Parks Departments, hotels, cruise ships, and anywhere one might wish to hide advertise Wi-Fi connectivity. The world over has embraced this new world without reservation. New devices are released annually by the major players in the arena of technology with new applications released almost daily to make our searches easier and our lifestyles more productive. Binge watching however is a practice which warrants an even closer look at how we spend time. The ability to binge watch an entire season in a single weekend leads to a wide array of physical and mental problems. Still there is no official study proving this to be true. What constitutes a person wanting to subject themselves to the same show for an inordinate amount of time? Perhaps it is the concept that we the viewer control how we want to watch something. Our willingness to view a show on commercialized television warrants we accept a barrage of advertising that in part takes away from the viewing pleasure we want to have after a long hard day at work. The television networks still privy to controlling how we watch a show no longer have a say as to when we watch it. If we DVR a certain show, most likely we will fast forward through the commercials. If we view the same show on a premium channel viewed on Demand we have to accept that our remote controls do not allow us to fast forward. It is then easy to assume many viewers wait for a show to be released on services like NETFLIX and HULU. There is a strange difference between these two heavyweights of customer viewing options. NETFLIX is absolute commercial free and most times if left alone one episode of a show will automatically roll in to another until the software prompts the viewer if they wish to continue watching the show. With a simple click on "Continue Watching" the binge viewing continues. On HULU when watching movies there are no commercial interruptions, however when watching a TV oriented show commercials interrupt the viewing and like with premium channel on demand shows the remote is made obsolete.

At the current time there are two services in direct competition for viewers wishing to go the route of controlled binge watching: APPLE TV and Amazon Direct. Both require the viewer to purchase a separate device connected to their TVs over Wi-Fi. Once connected the devices supply the viewer with connectivity to computer generated services like YOUTUBE and SkyNews. A person connected through these devices can view their shows with minimum interruptions monitored by these giants of technology. The future generations will more than likely have more options for viewing shows at their leisure than can be imagined today. Suffice to say the idea of escaping from our daily routines no longer includes separating ourselves from technology. Several ads for different products display family's waiting in line for vacations at airports wherein the parents advise they may not have Wi-Fi where they are going. The reaction from their children is widespread panic. Communicating face-to-face has been compromised since the advent of the Internet, with changes although minimal in nature continue to further separate us from one another. Whether it is binge watching and the doors locked to the outside world or the fear of having to talk to one another; we are cultivating a practice for the sake of personal convenience that promises to have many different effects for us later. Another commercial displays children being left at their grandparents house and the father advising them to be polite despite there being nothing much to do. Once inside the grandmother advises they have a new cable system with faster uploads and Wi-Fi friendly. The kids are elated which includes asking their parents if they could sleep over at Nana's house. Any and all future advances will further embellish how we stand a chance of being thought entertaining or cool enough to have our grandchildren want to spend time with us.

ADMINISTRATIVE TECHNOLOGY SYNDROME

One can easily make the conclusion we do not have a firm grasp on how technology is utilized today. The information collected to facilitate any company in every industry is by far the best means of supporting the company's policies are being adhered to. However, when the information is used to monitor an employee's capabilities there are serious flaws in how the system functions. A terminology should be affixed to those in management who sit at their desks using computer generated reports to define their staff. The term Administrative Technology Syndrome could define these kinds of managers. Before technology was the mainstay of corporations and facilities managers were responsible for getting to know their staff on a one-on-one basis. The computer generated files in use by most businesses creates a digital profile of what an employee does on a daily basis - leaving the manager a ways and means of accepting the computers data as the only trait defining whether the company has a good or bad worker. This practice is becoming more prevalent in service related jobs where computer reports seriously hinder the true value of a workers commitment. In the medical industry more and more administrators allow themselves to become bogged down in reports eliminating the entire experience of knowing their staff individually. In many respects the applications utilized in the medical profession adhere to properly controlling every aspect of a patient's experience. The demands placed on staff personnel to maintain patient care while updating computers every step of the way diminishes the quality of care in favor of satisfying computer generated protocols. A.T.S. as I am defining the problem stems from more and more hospitals wanting to look good on paper - or in this case according to their projected standards in a database. The downside to this mindset is causing problems throughout the medical industry because the key workers (nurses / doctor) are expected to spend more of their valuable time filling out computer questionnaires regarding patient status throughout their shifts. The primary victims of this practice are nurses who spend close to an hour sometimes more per shift to update and certify each patient's upkeep. In doing so their managers spend as much if not more time assuring the data is compliant with every patients care. In theory this is done to assure the highest level of patient care; however the data cannot be superseded by the actual realistic circumstances each nurse is exposed to. For generations nursing was considered "a calling" whereby the individual who chose to become a nurse was considered by many to be a caregiver of the highest regard. Since the advent of technology, nursing has in many ways required these dedicated individuals to manage a person's care while maintaining a digital footprint that follows the patient from admittance to their going home. This serves as a best case scenario when all the information is carefully documented every step of the way. However, given the number of patients nurses have to assist a formula for disaster enters in to the equation. On any given day, a nurse could find herself overwhelmed by the care one patient may require during her shift. Multiply the number of patients requiring extra care and it stands to reason why hospitals feel a need to define themselves as sufficient or delinquent in taking care of their patients. Most times it has little to do with nursing capabilities, but more so in how fewer and fewer administrators care to go beyond computer generated reports to monitor their staffs. The problem when collecting data to assist in following a patient's progress is two-fold. First and foremost if all is done properly in accordance with computer generated expectations and the actual care a patient receives the hospital does it job. However, if any way a patient's digital profile is not up to date with their carbon footprint, the issue of the kind of care received becomes questionable. For example, in the event a nurse has 8 patients and each patient requires 3 medications - every medication given out has to be updated in a database. On one hand this affords the hospital a way of monitoring inventory. On the other hand it affirms the nurse is doing their job in accordance with doctor's orders. However when medications are required on an hourly basis the care required in one area of a nurses section can become backed up or in some cases easily missed. It is by Administrative standards unacceptable for a nurse to miss any step during any shift. The ability to maintain a perfect computer generated profile for hospital purposes versus a perfect reputation for taking care of patients is a constant issue in most hospitals. To facilitate the best care possible for every patient, administrators need to evaluate their staff on a human scale and not a computer generated one. Using the medical profession to define ATS is by far the most crucial industry where computerized information affects the outcome of everyday life. There is a life and death scenario which represents the highest level of care to task ratio. Other industries utilizing the same method of monitoring computer profiles over that of employee potential strengthens the belief we no longer have a firm grasp as to how work is done, only that it be done in accordance with computerized levels of satisfaction. What is thought to be a tool for optimizing productivity serves only to slow down human capabilities in a reasonable time frame. Scanning, filing, maintaining reports are only some of the daily activities workers are expected to exhibit as a job skill in the modern world. The actual capability of what needs to be accomplished gets lost when data dictates any workers capability. Reliance on technology to define a machines performance does not cross over to the same standards for humans. While this can sound tedious in some ways, those individuals graded on whether they performed certain tasks throughout their work day, taking in to account only those things the computer reports they did not do caters to very primitive understanding of any job. Nowhere in any reports does hindrances come in to the equation. In a hospital setting if someone's medication is not given out in an allotted time frame, it is necessary for the administrators to fully investigate the reasons. In any service related job if a scan is not made at a particular time, here too unless the missing of these points becomes chronic; administrators have to get up from behind their desks and find out what is causing any delays. The most obvious delays get lost when living by computer reports alone. Inclement weather plays a key role in diagnosing why something may be delayed. For an administrator to evaluate a person's performance against a computer's expectations defeats the purpose of managing his / her staff in a proper manner. The alienation between management and employee is compromised when the dignity factor is erased. Those managers who suffer from ATS most times have no regard for making improvements. Instead they abide by the computer reports to distinguish their daily workload. Efficiency will continue to diminish the company's productivity and moral when managers cannot communicate with the staff.

SPRING FEVER

We are an amusing species. After the coldest of winters filled with record breaking temperatures below zero and snowfalls estimated to be the largest in recent memory; mankind comes out of hibernation sensing they have survived what bears appreciate knowing once the spring thaw commences. Drifts of snow piled waist high the day before reduced to clumps of ice in the blink of an eye. If science lessons in school served us well, condensation increases with heat and the elements once thought overwhelming disappear. Nature is an incredible testament to the changes in disposition and comfort. Those who live in "warm only" climates do not fully experience the changing of seasons. They embrace a complacency that warrants their daily activities threatened by rain in some parts or excessive heat in others. Only the places that experience the full four seasons can attest to the emotions associated to weather. In recent years a term has been adopted by the medical profession whereby individuals can experience mood changes related to the weather. The term is comical and brilliant at the same time – Seasonal Affect Disorder or

S.A.D. which gives way to the different ways people react to the changes in temperature. Over the course of one's life time we inevitably become affected by the elements around us. Still nothing prepares us for the ways people react once the warmer air arrives. People thought distraught and unable to cope with life's expectations suddenly feel more alive than they thought possible. Strange things happen when the thermometer climbs above a certain degree – some people regain their composure and as many lose their minds. The change over from Cabin Fever to Spring Fever can cause catastrophic results in the human condition. Most times it is confined to one's change in attitude, and often times it results in bouts of extreme actions. Take for example the woman who purchased at the end of summer a new bathing suit. The second it appears the sun is shining with a level of warmth, she puts on the bathing suit and lounges in her yard – sunglasses on and tan oil spread everywhere. Shoes many purchased at discount prices appear on their feet allowing them to strut instead of tiptoeing over mounds of snow. The male of the species reacts in different ways. He begins to disrobe at levels that display bare shoulders under tank tops and here too they strut with a longer stride. In big cities the Spring Fever phenomenon results in a fashion extravaganza nobody was ready to witness. The blacks, browns and dark blues explode in to yellows, oranges and bright reds. Boots if worn at all are knee high with an air of look at me persona. Nothing quite prepares us for spring. The weather channels seem to go in to a period of mourning no longer capable of scaring the bejesus out of viewers. Clear skies and higher temperatures do not make for a good weatherman's prognosis. They live for the words "storm" and "disaster." They inevitably start researching their computer databases for new ways to bring back their audience. In the wake of Spring Fever they study their weather models in hopes of mapping summer time disasters. Words crop in to their daily reporting like "tsunami" and "earthquakes." But mankind prevails through these seasons without inkling to look back. Except for those people who saw their towns devastated by climate the seasons change with a calm introduction to the days ahead. The fury in some people's steps causes them to lose sight they have not had the liberty of walking as fast as they now suddenly can. Their legs are akin to those individuals who spent a long time at sea. Getting used to the landscape takes some doing. A few never admit the change in their mood or ability to deal with the changes. These people are the same ones who never have to pick up leaves in autumn or shovel snow in winter. The elements are a nuisance on a different wavelength for them. Time moves on and what was a revelation of spiritual proportions one day gets taken for granted the next. New things crop up that we humans find fault with on a daily basis. We cannot help ourselves. While the rosy pictures of daily life are reported on Facebook, the actual realities of our lives confront the issues that force us to balance our existence. The checks and balances of our income always a concern becomes a focused upon reality as Tax Day – April 15th in America looms. The anxieties of how much snow we will get during a winter storm is replaced by how much will I owe Uncle Sam. People who are

SAD in many ways will always be SAD. It is a part of their DNA to focus on the negative when the positive is staring them in the face. As we age the levels of SAD become more pronounced as we go through cycles of health related deficiencies. Every man, woman and child is now categorized by their health related practices. Countless commercials bombard us every day on television, radio and newspaper ads. There is no escape from the body's seasons. We too go through seasons that last as long as we can attain a certain healthy outlook on life. Frank Sinatra's song "It Was a Very Good Year" is the best example for how seasons change in our lives. The song starts with the narrator at 17 years of age, carefree and wild in what we can only assume is the Spring of his life. As the song progresses the narrator turns 21 and 35 representing the Summer years. In the next stanza he is in the Autumn of his life and comparing himself to vintage wine. The winter of his life is not mentioned, it is in many ways a gamble as to how many people will actually live in to their winter years. At best, it is the Spring that embraces any chance of happiness according to the song's lyrics. In as much as we may take for granted the seasonal changes, we cannot deny that as we get older we tend to look over our shoulder more often. Maybe it was the illusion that yesterday was easier, giving way to the phrase every generation utters – "the good old days." So it is that we can compare our celebrations related to longer life spans due to medical discoveries and better living conditions. Or we can consider ourselves – lucky. Being born when we are born plays a key role in how we develop our innate personalities as humans. The astronomy industry makes a fortune off of proclaiming how our days will unravel according to the stars. The people who make a living off of daily horoscopes may be the best writers we as a species ever produced. They incorporate an air of optimism with a level of caution in less than 50 words every day. If the same people who write horoscopes could become weatherman we may have a fighting chance at immortality.

C.O.W.S AND PRISONERS

There are more C.O.W.'s than prisoners. The reason is rather simple; because every prisoner is a C.O.W. It is not a statistic easily maintained. Some Casualties of War never bother to register their pain. They live with the hidden sadness buried deep within them. Over the course of several years they get inklings of emotions that limit their ability to handle certain situations. Throughout the first decade of the 21st century more and more casualties are beginning to face their inner demons. I am not a psychiatrist or a therapist; I am like you a witness. The inability for too many in our society to cope with what we all saw becomes evident when we see and hear of individuals with a penchant to act out. Whether it is a single incident of some poor innocent child forced to reconcile with the images of violence or a group of individuals needing to lash out at one another for the sake of going viral; every one is the blame for ignoring what it means. In many respects we have adopted a phrase that explains away the problem; we say *they are desensitized.* Fostering the actions of individuals who are at war with their inability to face what we all saw does not constitute a reason for the sadness they face every day. It has been said every war creates orphans. Our orphans are not institutionalized; they are struggling in our neighborhoods to live with something they cannot comprehend. Those that carry on each day while seeking some balance inside no longer possible only begins to explain the widespread madness we have nurtured. On 9/11 what happened is not only about those that died, but in many cases more about those left behind. Too young to fully fathom what they lost, there is a direct correlation between seeing and believing. They saw it but it somehow remains in their minds an illusion. These victims try to fit in and desperately want to get past what so many were told to do hours after the attacks; get back to normal. Living in America is not only about the freedom of speech, freedom of the press; it is inevitably about our right to pursue happiness. But what if the pursuit is a problem for some people? What if individuals take the images and comprehend the solution, "get back to normal" as realization bad things can be easily ignored? They embrace an attitude they can get away with doing whatever they please and it does not mean anything. Much has been written in the 21st century about the ill effects of violent video games, increased violent films being made and the youth of our society embracing it all as comical entertainment. Since 2001 there have been more random acts of violence in our schools. There have been more incidents associated with individuals needing psychiatric attention because they cannot cope with their negative emotions. It has become cool to provoke violence so it can be videotaped and uploaded to the Internet. In both of these incidents, the mindset is one of seeking attention. These C.O.W.'s are crying out in the wilderness. We are allowing them to stray further and further from the safety they can no longer see in front of their eyes. Whether it is a single act of badgering innocent people, calling out names and inciting fear; or carrying out their interpretation of hitting another person to get a rise out of them – it is a problem we do not have an answer to remedy. Too many times we have seen young people in our society in self- created melees, captured on video and thrown onto social media sites. They do it not to condone the violence; they do it so they can be thought famous. Fame in this regard is an infamous kind of notoriety where by their actions are dismissed as violent in nature but more so as a means to seek attention. In an odd way it is the same infamous kind of notoriety sort by terrorist in the name of a blatant cause they deem worthy of promoting. We are nurturing our own terrorist who cannot make a distinction between what is reality and delusional mentality. I have no credentials that warrant me an ability to judge anyone. However, as a concerned citizen I believe we are blind to the reasons causing this behavior. It is easy to blame parents for lacking necessary disciple in the home. It is easier to blame the world these individuals are exposed to without proper explanation or guidance. These incidents of random acts of violence will inevitably escalate until they are the next excuse of getting back to normal as soon as possible. They will continue until we are all prisoners of our combined fears. Is there a solution?

Regions of sorrow, doleful shades, where peace
And rest can never dwell, hope never comes
John Milton – Paradise Lost

THE COSTA RICAN DIARIES

While attending a funeral I had the pleasure of meeting the son of the man who had died. The son and I had met briefly a few times when introduced by his father. During those meetings we talked about many things we both found interesting. On the top of our list was our admiration for the father who lived an amazing life. He had served in the military during WWII and went on to have a career in advertising and later as a clerk for the U.S. Post Office. In all of his endeavors he shared a love of music which he passed on to his son Robert. During our conversation at the funeral Robert used the phrase "The Jazz King" when talking about his memories of his father. Robert had an amazing life as well, choosing to pursue music as a career which allowed him entry in to the elite company of famous composers like Philip Glass and dance artists like Alvin Ailey. At the height of his success he opted to leave the hustle bustle of New York's arts and culture society and moved to Costa Rica. At the end of the services celebrating his father's life we made promises to stay in touch. When I went home that night I could not help but think of how much Robert admired his father. He admitted during one flurry of memories how he had separated himself numerous times from his father's life, desperately wanting to strike out on his own and make something of himself. The next morning after being up most of the night thinking of our conversation, I contacted Robert asking when he would be returning to Costa Rica. He advised me he would be heading back later in the week. I asked if he would tell more about his father and his decision to move. We agreed to meet at his sister's house later in the day. When I arrived he opted to sit in the yard telling me he had gotten used to the heat living where he did. In the yard our conversation picked up where it had the night before. I told him I had friends I knew my entire life who could not sit and have a conversation like the one we were sharing. He told me his decision to move to Costa Rica included the same revelation, how Americans can no longer just sit and enjoy good company. We sat listening to music on CDs I had brought with me and the flow of emotions related to his Dad's passing fed in to our connection. We both knew the same man in different ways but ended up admiring him the same way. I had the distinct pleasure of meeting him when my brother-in-law married Robert's sister. The combining of family's can sometimes offer amazing surprises. Robert's father Richard and I hit it off immediately. He had a sense of humor that left anyone in his company hysterical. Much of his observations came with a knack of poking fun at the world around us. I could not help but agree with nearly everything he said. When it came to talking about jazz, his eyes seemed to light up like a pinball machine. Suddenly the

stories were pouring out of him like a waterfall. During his
years of musical discovery he had the experience of meeting
some of the biggest names in Jazz. He told tales of sitting with
them after gigs at the Village Vanguard and Birdland.
Listening to the energy in his voice when talking about jazz
was like hearing an encyclopedia come to life. His love of life
was second to none and his enthusiasm and love for family
was unlike anything I ever heard or witnessed. Having lost
my father when I was 18 years old, I was in awe of anyone
who had experienced such a full and satisfying life. In his later
years he was diagnosed with Alzheimer's, which is in my
opinion one of the worst diseases known to man. Despite his
ailing memory he never lost his spark for enjoying life. When I
visited him as the disease worsened he had gotten it in his
head we were war buddies. I mentioned in passing to him
several times that we had being in the military in common. I
served during the Vietnam War and for whatever reason what
war did not matter when his memories started to fade. War is
war as the saying goes. During those meetings I could not
help but be thrilled to hear him telling me how we both
enjoyed discovering different things in Europe during the
war. Mostly I would stir the conversation to music and again
the same glow came in to his eyes that I first witnessed.
During his recollections of music I got to be the friend who sat

on a bar stool next to him as Fats Waller played on the stage. I got to be the guy who didn't know who Louis Armstrong was when he sat next to us at the Village Vanguard. I learned to keep my mouth shut and play right along with the memories. The kinds of memories I wish were real. The kind of spirit I wish I had known longer. When Robert left New York returning to Costa Rica we promised to stay in touch. I asked his sister for his address and wrote a book size letter to him. Several weeks passed and a book size letter from him came in response. I sent an email message after getting his address and suggested we continue writing. In the email message I also recommended we only communicate via handwritten letters. He agreed that sounded more interesting than the coldness of electronic mail. The intensity of the letters turned in to journal sized composition note books and designer diaries I purchased for the sole purpose of having something unique to send him. He built a bookshelf to house the growing library which he deemed The Costa Rican Diaries. To fully understand what writing has become and what it once was, only an experience like The Costa Rican Diaries can offer a definition. The diaries because they are strictly handwritten have no life beyond the time they are written and read.

Once received from Robert I place my copies in a special draw in my desk. Robert as mentioned places his on shelves he built. There is a free spirit quality related to writing in a way that people wrote before the invention of the Internet. It takes on a deliberate connection to writing as an art form whether or not anything is actually of any interest except to the two people writing. What the Internet has done is erase the personalized quality of actually physically connecting pen to paper. One might argue the same experience can be had between two individuals who send messages back and forth via email. I would argue the experience is by no means comparative because the instantaneous exchange of email messages warrants a different mindset when reading or writing. What the diaries have is a separated quality that is written in response to something received that will not have a chance at being responded to for weeks sometimes months later. This may sound ridiculous to people in need of instant gratification. I would argue gratification has little to do with the experience. During our exchanges we inevitably got around to sharing memories. What we discovered was how small the world. When discussing my childhood memories of living in Glendale mentioning Forest Park; Robert counted with his own recollections of growing up in Richmond Hill and his memories of Forest Park. He shared his thoughts about the same streets I knew in my neighborhood like Myrtle Avenue, Woodhaven Boulevard, Jamaica Avenue and it started to get eerie when we realized we went to the same high school. Several years ago I read a book entitled, Two Prospectors: The Letters of Sam Shepard and Johnny Dark. Sam Shepard is a famous American playwright and Johnny Dark is a friend who was once Shepard's father-in-law. For four decades Shepard and Dark wrote letters, taped conversations and exchanged insights on every conceivable topic known to man. It is considered a fascinating study in friendship and artistic pursuit. Robert and I are only in our first decade of the Costa Rican Diaries. We have what amounts to a special friendship all part of the Jazz King's legacy. Here's the tidbit that we both wish to make a shared project one day, we want to tell the Jazz King's life story. Before his memory started to fade he spent nights dictating his life story to his wife Chris who as luck would have it, bothered to write it down. What a remarkable gift she gave Richard in listening beyond hearing. Taking the time to put in down for eternity. *The Jazz King Was Here!* There are also elements of the Costa Rican Diaries that could never have been experienced if we dumped messages in to our electronic mailboxes; Robert has the worst handwriting known to mankind! With that said, I can decipher every word like I taught myself to read a foreign language. He has to tolerate my tangents when writing free-hand which result sometimes in 20 page diatribes about the weather. I tried what I call a shared-journal writing project in the past with several people. Inevitably I realized this kind of writing is not for everyone. As time goes by there is a sense of *being lost* related to commenting on something or responding to an event which by the time you get around to writing is long past. I made the mistake in one journal to comment about Henry Miller's work not being up to snuff. I awakened in Robert a kind of ire not experienced in prior diaries. It was in many respects a manifesto that I had no idea what I was talking about. He was right! It forced me to look deeper in to Miller's work discovering he is not only about his two well - known books, Tropic of Cancer and Tropic of Capricorn. My limited exposure to Miller's work opened a can of worms which was absolutely delightful! Robert's tour de force diary sent to me caused an avalanche of memories which further celebrated his father's legacy. Miller's books were banned in the United States for a period of time and Richard during WWII got his hands on copies available in Europe. It was those copies that Robert received from his father. It was those copies that opened up in him a yearning for artistic fervor. This is an amazing legacy for a son to have from his father.

The Costa Rican Diaries will never see the light of day. Their sole purpose is an exchange of thoughts, ideas and concepts about the human condition. They are a cherished part of my library that no one will ever read except me.

ADIRONDACK CHAIRS

It has come to my attention that Americans have been inundated with too many choices. Choice is advertised as a wonderful freedom giving people options that offer them exposure to different things. For the sake of a short history lesson, we of a certain age did not always enjoy this freedom of choice. This recent phenomenon has come about because technology will stop at nothing to provide us with more features and more applications and more ways of doing everything. While I can appreciate advancements in certain areas of our benefits with choices; a serious problem occurs when things go too far. When mentioning certain things related to choice a person risks being categorized as over a certain age. This happens during discussions about music, movies, television shows and books. Despite the great leaps forward in the medical profession, allowing people to look and stay younger longer; we lose our cover when endorsing our taste in music. Even if the new breed of everything from the past is cool for selling us cars, corn flakes and new devices; inevitably our age is discovered. I can live with that. When discussing movies most times I blow my cover in less time it takes a politician to say I promised you that, but I did not know about this. The movies I enjoyed growing up had plots with maybe 15 minutes of special effects; while today special effects are listed in the credits as a character in the movie.

Again, I can live with that. On television the biggest leap in technology has come in to our living rooms. Many of us still call the big screen object in our homes a television; it is not a television. It is a big screen object capable of downloading – uploading – streaming – broadcasting – connecting – saving – sharing – and so on. I had at best on a good day 10 channels when growing up. Seven local stations and 3 that came in on UHF which was a frequency associated with people who swore they were abducted by aliens. Given the choices today, the average person under the age of 40 has never known a world so primitive. I can live with that. In the world of books, the advances are again commendable. Under the auspices of saving trees and using the environment in a way that convinces people they are saving the planet; books are being slowly eliminated from our world. Predictions estimate book stores will be a thing of the past in 20 years. Have you read Fahrenheit 451 by Ray Bradbury? I won't go in to the plot of the book – suffice to say it is a must read for any civilized human being. The point being we are eliminating the existence of physical books in support of a digital facsimile. I have a problem with that. But I digress this is not about things that date me; it is about Adirondack chairs. People please consider the risk of demoralizing this artifact of our past? Few people know the Adirondack chair is a New York based invention; made by a gentleman named Thomas Lee while vacationing in Westport, New York way back there in 1903. Consider the fact that Mr. Lee's only desire was to provide a comfortable chair for his family. After several attempts at the design he shared his invention with a local carpenter down on his luck. The carpenter Harry Bunnell filed for a patent and became rich selling the chairs for the next twenty years of his life. The Adirondack chair is perhaps the first case of stolen ideas being taken right from beneath our noses! One could argue that Harry Bunnell that scoundrel of 20th century chair-related crimes was the first entrepreneur who did not take things sitting down! This innovative furniture design became a staple at resorts and country clubs around the world. The original design called for two colors: green and medium dark brown. This is where I feel we need to make a stand! A few years ago the chairs started appearing in different colors. They started to appear in bright colors like "get me sunglasses yellow" and the shameless "are you embarrassed yet red" or the most despicable use of "looks like a seashell turquoise." First we as cultivated humans had to accept the chairs being made out of plastic instead of the original design of 11 wooden planks. What have we allowed to happen to the world! I understand the upcoming months of deciding who will run our country, and the importance of whether a favorite television show gets picked up for a new season on Netflix; but people I am talking about comfort here. I am discussing the very foundation of where we park our butts! How can you stand by and worry about promises that never happen or whether we will ever know what happens after The Big Bang Theory and Friends are no longer available as reruns! People this is about our sense of common decency! Do you not want to have a say about the dignity of our nation's future? I hereby nominate the Adirondack chair as the official chair of the planet earth. I will immediately begin my campaign by promising you the chair will be aboard the first official spaceship to land on Mars. I have sent a petition to NASA and members of Congress who enjoy sitting on their asses – that we the American people want what is best for the future of mankind. I have asked talented photographers and painters to submit samples of their work displaying two Adirondack chairs facing the planet earth from the surface of Mars. In those chairs I wish to include the most natural of all things Adirondack – a copy of one book on each chairs arm representing a love of the past for the sake of tomorrow. To eradicate the national debt I am suggesting a special lottery be created allowing people to bet on which books will be chosen. The lottery will take place upon liftoff of the spaceship "Adirondack I" sometime before the end of this century. We can idle our time arguing about who deserves to wear designer suits standing in front of microphones talking about things that stay the same no matter who wins or we can make a difference by standing united for the sake of one day sitting down and enjoying a setting sun. Sadly, in closing it is my belief we can talk about idealisms related to world peace, ending world hunger, discovering cures for diseases or we can be realistic and embrace a cause that gives actual meaning to our having been here as a species. Candidates for "Adirondack I" will be conducted in a nationally televised reality show airing on channels everywhere. Early leading names for the show: Don't Just Sit There! And Sit Down and Shut Up have caused a buzz in Hollywood. We can do this America!

A BRIEF HISTORY OF PRIVACY

Walking home one afternoon after school I noticed a group of kids laughing as I got closer. My first inclination was to look behind me followed by checking to see if I had forgotten to dress properly as gym was my final class. Assured their laughing had nothing to do with me I started walking toward them not caring what was so funny. The closer I got, the louder their laughter which included pointing at me. A girl in the group said, "Here comes the neighborhood loser!" I had no idea what they were talking about and I passed by them feeling embarrassed. When I got home my brother was sitting at the kitchen table looking distraught. He told me a bunch of kids were calling him a loser all day in school. When I told him what happened to me we both became highly suspicious. Children no matter how much they are taught to respect others have a tendency to take what they hear and use it as a means of ammunition. For several weeks we both had the same experience walking home from school. What could have caused our reputations to turn in to symbols of public scrutiny? It was a mystery we lived with until one day the most casual of activities turned out to be the source of our indignity. While sitting in the living room I overheard my mother talking while hanging clothes out to dry. Back then every apartment in the neighborhood had a clothesline that stretched to poles in people's backyards. Getting up to see who she could be talking to further unraveled the mystery. Sticking my head out the living room window I saw at least a dozen women hanging their clothes as well with enough shouting taking place to almost cover my ears. I informed my brother about my discovery and we started to piece together the puzzle that was the bane of our existence. Our mother was saying things that she had no idea could be used against us. It took several more clothes hanging days to figure out exactly what happened. We sat near the open window in the living room listening to the banter going back and forth and up and down the backyard network of rumors and neighborhood chit-chat. One afternoon my mother said what we needed to hear. After a woman two houses down remarked how her son had lost his lunch money, our mother responded by saying, "Well you know my two; they're losing things all the time." Her proclamation was followed by laughter and a rousing series of clothespins being dropped in to the yards below. We both confronted my mother advising her she needed to stop saying things to the neighbors when hanging our clothes. She had no idea what we were talking about and promptly punished us for what she felt was disrespectful. A harmless statement made in passing about our tendency to misplace things had made us the brunt of neighborhood jokes. In retrospect my brother and I may have lost a few things in our youth, like school supplies, our school ties or a pencil or two; but in no way did that make us losers in the conventional sense of the word. During those years of backyard routines, neighbors, mostly women owned the ways and means of how information was shared. The misinterpretation of information passed on in conversation in different homes created the first sensation we hear about today related to cyberbullying. In most cases it happens when a child overhears something said by an adult which gets twisted in to a factual reason for making fun of others. Knowledge as the saying goes is power. When my brother and I realized our mother was the source of our public humiliation we set about to even the score. For days after our discovery of this pipeline of humility we sat by the living room window whenever our mother was hanging clothes. We could have filled up notebooks with the repartee happening outside. One day coming home from school as we passed the clique of classroom gossipers we stopped in front of them and started our barrage of newly discovered ammunition. "Oh yeah, well did you know Suzy likes to sleep with her parents because she's afraid of the dark? And "Billy has a bed wetting problem which is why his mother has to hang his sheets out to dry every morning!" We were just warming up as we had heard enough to retaliate against each kid. When we were finished with our defense there was a loud silence. We told the group of kids how we had heard about each of their private issues and a truce was declared. One girl responded by saying, "I lose my school supplies all the time. It's not intentional and it doesn't make me a loser." Girls despite every level of comparison when I was growing up understood things easier and better. We guys were too busy being boys. There was a saying which over time made the best sense as to how those early years of information sharing came to be, "you're acting like a bunch of wash women." In our modern world the sharing of information is made easier than household chores. A person can make a comment which can be totally misconstrued and ends up causing the same results. We have graduated from the backyard banter to an everywhere is the battlefield mentality. Postings on Facebook and Twitter advertise our malcontent for certain agencies like daily sanitation pick-up and a casual comment about their being late. This can be turned in to an attack on garbage men who it just so happens is married to the next door neighbor. Which results in a defense of how hard they work and who the hell are you to complain having more garbage than the entire neighborhood put together! Or the comments made against local government officials on a page where the curator is an official. The list goes on and on today in different ways for every age group. Ridiculous things like who owns a parking space after someone digs their car out after a storm. The comments can stretch in to infinity regarding the rights of one individual over another. It is nothing more than our tendency as human beings to share our opinion and stories. In the same way our privacy which we want to protect at all cost is bleeding from our fingertips as we type away our belief we have friends hiding behind the wash-lines coming from our homes every day. An age old cliché sums it up perfectly, "the more things change, the more they remain the same." We can be given tools to communicate with other planets and inevitably our natural tendency to broadcast our opinions will surface. Privacy today is the real joke. Every sign-on and keystroke dictates our daily activities. We have become our own advertisers making it easier for companies to sell us everything under the sun. We are our own worst enemies when thinking we can hide behind a screenname on a social media site. We subscribe to other people's wash lines and in doing so we end up sharing anything we think might be interesting. We provide fodder for the neighborhood organizations that can use the comments we make as a ways and means to facilitate our schools. Our unity on any proposals for change in the neighborhood can be seen as a form of contempt. An entire community can be labeled prejudice or against something based entirely on hearsay and misplaced rhetoric. In the process we all become losers in the conventional sense. We have lost our understanding of what it means to keep our opinions guarded in mixed company. Nowhere else is there more of a mixed company population than while online. Many people in our society believe they are privately sharing their thoughts with "friends." The word is all consuming. It brings about a psychological emotion of safety. However, unless we actually know all 2068 friends we accumulated on Facebook, it is best to stay clear about who loses what in your home. Our natural want for attention is so engrained in us; we have lost the ability to censor our own thoughts. Also much to our shared fears there are individuals who collect our data to actually steal our identities. They can easily accumulate a profile about us by monitoring the things we say in passing. There is a world-wide network of thieves who take our comments and construct an entirely new persona for anyone seeking to become someone else. In recent years a new form of privacy is at risk under the tag-line of seeking help. Parents looking for answers as to why Suzy is afraid of the dark or why Billy wets his bed will publicly solicit information. The term currently defining this activity is "Sharenting." People seeking answers with an innocent intention of finding something out about their children are using a public forum to advertise each problem they may be experiencing. There are people who champion this form of parental exchange because they in many ways are too busy to find answers from a more reliable source. The examples of how our privacy is no longer a viable means of defining our security is as easy as sitting by an open living room window and listening to the neighbors hanging their laundry.

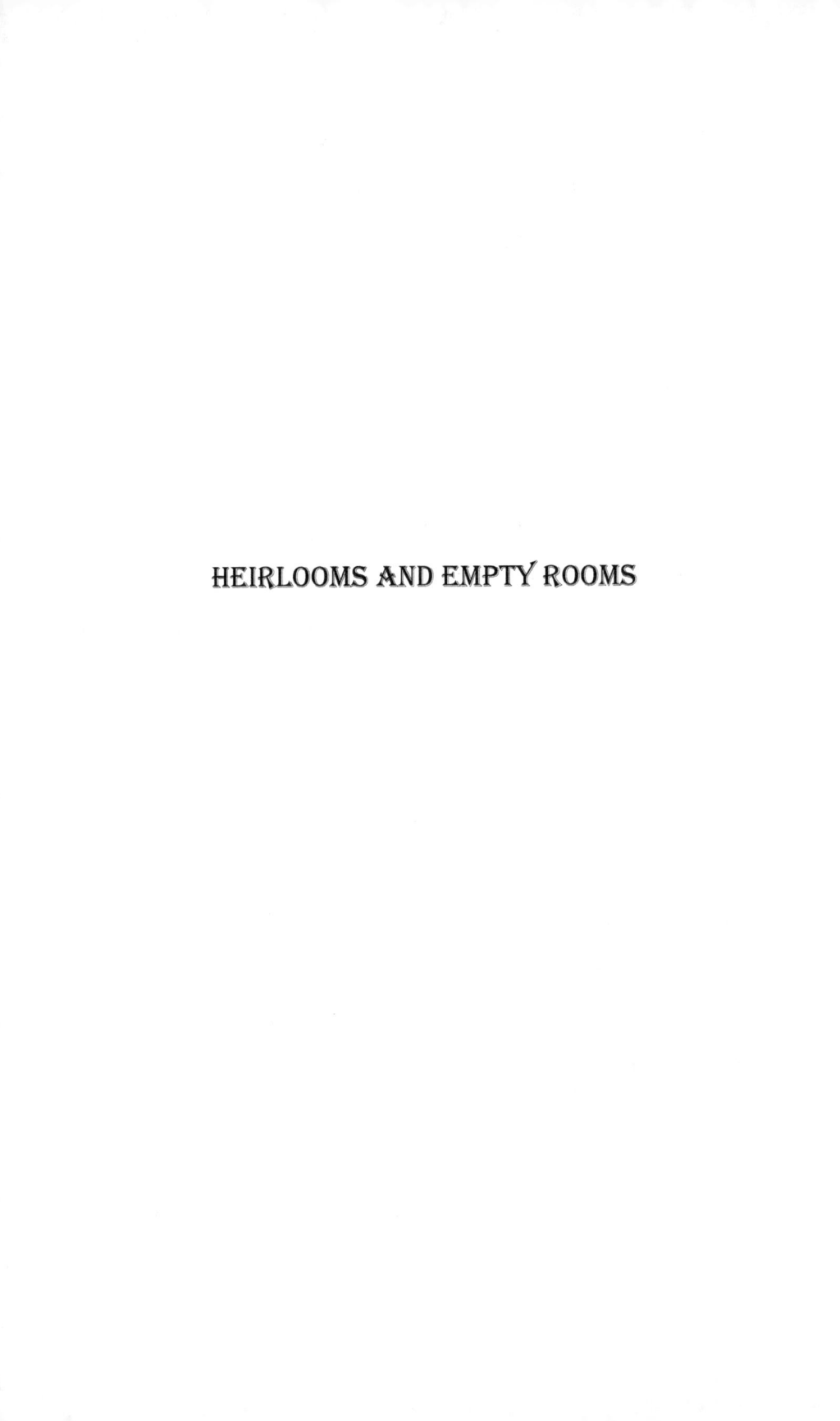

HEIRLOOMS AND EMPTY ROOMS

Is the thought of having something besides money remotely appealing to families? Having spent time cleaning out a loved one's house, was it disappointing for me to discover nothing of value? Did nothing inside a house amount to anything beyond old furniture or a hideous lamp not suitable for shining light? Was I expecting to find something? Did I feel a need to have something that represented a family history? The process took weeks and in the end after a sidewalk sale, the house was empty and the rooms seemed to echo with conversations. Is it possible the empty rooms were the legacy I needed to listen to? Some heirlooms have no material value or the thought of them belonging to someone else keeps us attached to the most ridiculous things. Maybe this is not as important as I make it out to be. A lot of people can uproot and move to new faraway places, selling everything they own. They have a capability to start fresh without looking back. Or is there something more complicated about their going that deserves silence? Perhaps it is better not knowing if moving away from everything you knew provides comfort you never had. If the empty rooms some place new awaiting fresh beginnings can give you a sense of happiness than allow yourself to start over. However, what if the getting away is not part of the equation, and you live a few blocks from the loved one's house, or several miles at best and the roots you call your own rely on staying put? Is it possible memories are the common man's heirloom? If so, why don't last will and testaments include space for memoirs? Enough space so the children, dearest relative or friend can know what is worth keeping? Would that be considered proper etiquette to leave something more important than the baseball signed by Derek Jeter? Or more valuable than the silverware kept in that box the family only saw on holidays? Or the diamond necklace and earrings worn by a grandmother on her wedding day? Or that vase in the china closet taken out once a year to display flowers from the garden? How comforting to realize we have the Antique Roadshow to help us put a monetary value on things from our past. But who puts a true value on our past if memories get forgotten or can be easily misplaced? I had a strange experience of visiting my childhood home one day. I was driving with a friend on the avenue where I once lived and passed the apartment I spent the majority of growing up. The friend noticed the door was open and the apartment was under construction. He pulled the car over and we entered the house. Everything I knew was gone, the walls and floors had been gutted leaving just the staircase left standing. Without the walls the space looked immense. Without the floors the space looked expansive. There was a loud cooing noise coming from the top of the stairs. I had lived on the top floor and my immediate reaction after entering was to climb the stairs. At the top of the landing I looked up to where my room once had been and saw pigeons nesting in the rafters. I hollered to my friend who opted to inspect the first floor advising him there were pigeons in my room. His response was a comical reminder to cover my head. Standing there for a moment I tried to listen for any hint of things my family may have left behind. Realizing it was rather too sentimental to expect anything, I noticed a ladder in the space that led to the roof. It had to be the same rickety ladder that was once housed in a little closet outside my room. A ladder I climbed many times to take in the view of the avenue and the park across the street. From atop the house on a clear night you could see clear in to Manhattan. The Twin Towers standing majestic like mountains in the distance. There was a blinking red light atop one of the towers sending out what my young mind thought were Morse code messages to the moon. Standing on top of the world that was mine as a child I could see for miles. I could see into the park where lovers sat on benches and several chose to walk their dogs singing songs without headphones or concern anyone could hear them. Beyond the edge of the park was the highway with cars going by; if I closed my eyes the rubber tires made a sound similar to waves coming ashore on a beach. My friend yelled up to me advising we leave; he had to remind me we were technically trespassing. Back in the car he asked if I saw anything except the pigeons. I told him I had seen the ladder to the stars.

ONLY IN AMERICA

One of the biggest misconceptions for most people living in the U.S.A. has much to do with often used phrase "politically correct." The phrase is tossed around whenever we experience something that is not to our liking. Over the course of time when researching the origins of the phrase, it appears to have been mentioned as far back as the 18th century, when in 1793 the Supreme Court used the phrase to discuss the proper means of defining the people of the United States over just saying United States. I have no idea what the difference might mean but it gave birth to a phrase that comes up every four years when we elect new leaders. Having researched the origins of the phrase it became obvious we need look no further than the song lyrics of one song from the 1960s – *Only in America*. When looking up the origins of this song which came in to prominence sung by a popular group – Jay and The Americans; we discover controversy prevailed related to how this one song contradicts our understanding about being people of the United States. It is not my intention to discuss politics by discussing this lyric, but perhaps somethings cannot be avoided. First it is important to discuss how the song came to be sung by Jay and the Americans.

The song originally had different lyrics and was written to be sung by another popular band of the era named The Drifters. During the hey-day of early rock and roll there was a very formulaic manner in which certain songs became popular. The formula sound we hear today is far different from the songs of the 1960s, but someone could argue not much has changed in how music becomes synonymous with its time. The original lyrics written by Jerry Leiber, Mike Stoller, Barry Mann and Cynthia Weil refer to a time in our past history when our cultural differences were thought to be at an all-time peak. Despite emotions related to segregation and integration nowhere else except on the radio can we trace the war that was being waged against the origins of racism. The vast majority of individuals who embraced the music of Chuck Berry, Little Richard, and Elvis Presley cared very little about who was singing the songs that made them feel the spirit of rock and roll. However, the leaders in certain states felt it was their duty to protect the people of the United States from this unlikely source of music as a tool of the devil. Oh how far we have traveled since those early days of rock radio. This essay is not about discussing the error or our ways when attempting to censor musical artist from our shared airwaves. After all we are a dignified and democratic society and stuff like that obviously never happened according to new historians. The original lyrics of the song *Only In America* challenged the very foundation of what was thought to be cool. The original lyric which was banned for years: "*Only in America, land of opportunity, can they save a seat in the back of the bus just for me. Only in America, Where they preach the Golden Rule, will they start to march when my kids go to school.*" It is quite obvious such lyrics in the 1960s would have caused a few people to lose sleep. However, when the song did make it to the airwaves by Jay and the Americans, another injustice was echoed that is part of our history to this day. The much more accepted sentiment in the revised version advises us that anyone can wake up to be President. By a show of hands, how many people alive today in the United States believe this to be true? We can openly release films that display the ignorance of our forefathers who embraced a philosophy of prejudice but we cannot openly discuss the fact that very few people can pursue the presidency. Today, we have a hidden agenda in America where only those privies to an elite background can attempt becoming the President of the United States. What this translates to is a higher disregard for the rights of all citizens despite their ethnic or religious background. This song with its complete history stands as a testimonial to how far we have come as a civilized nation. Despite your belief the song has a catchy sound with a positive message, nothing points to the possibility of anyone having a chance to become President. Instead, we will experience an entire year (2016) arguing which candidate best exemplifies the interest and concerns of the people of the United States. Names of family's who have had their chance to lead us will be bandied about because here in America we like the connection to celebrity status over that of which is important to our well-being as a united people. In retrospect the original lyric was in my opinion not in keeping with the dance floor mentality of the era. However relevant the intention of the writers, they were being politically involved where only the beat was necessary to cause a hit. And yet, their fixed lyric vowing anyone could become President is more of a lie then the stupidity of primitive uses of prejudicial ignorance. Every American should be made aware that no matter whether we are white, black, red or yellow – unless you have the backing of a very rich power oriented machine behind you, your chances of becoming President are next to impossible. The average Joe Public who may be a born leader need only apply as a candidate for running a local soup kitchen. Any higher ambition requires he or she sell their soul to the same devil linked to early rock music. In the meantime, the song itself stands as a pivotal example for lies that never get told beyond a good song with a danceable beat. Only in America.

Craig Schwab is the author of the novel "Something in the Neighborhood of Real" along with books of short stories – Tales from the Couch and a 40 year retrospective (1973-2013) on changes in America written with his life-long friend Tom Huber. He lives with his wife and three children in Glendale, New York. He can be reached via email: Kiddrane@aol.com

www.ingramcontent.com/pod-product-compliance
Lightning Source LLC
Chambersburg PA
CBHW070354290526

45790CB00004B/1490